WELCOME THE WORD

WELCOME THE WORD

Celebrating
the Liturgy of the Word
with children

Joan Brown SND

Illustrated by Arthur Baker

GEOFFREY
CHAPMAN

Geoffrey Chapman
An imprint of Cassell Publishers Limited
Villiers House, 41/47 Strand, London WC2N 5JE

First published 1989
Reprinted 1990, 1992, 1993

British Library Cataloguing in Publication Data

Brown, Joan
Welcome the Word; celebrating the Liturgy of the
Word with children.
   1. Catholic Church. Public worship
   I. Title
   264'.02

ISBN 0-225-66525-5

Typeset by Fons et Culmen
Printed and bound in Great Britain by The Bath Press

CONTENTS

ORDINARY TIME, YEAR B

ORDINARY TIME, YEAR C

OTHER FEASTS AND CELEBRATIONS

FOREWORD

Providing children with a Liturgy of the Word is to be very much encouraged. Many members of the worshipping community are children. They are important members of the Church and as such should be helped to prepare to take a full part in the Sunday liturgy.

The Church is responsible for the spiritual and liturgical formation of her children, and providing them with their own Liturgy of the Word is one important way of fulfilling this obligation.

It would seem fitting that where children attend adult liturgy in our churches every Sunday, they should be provided with a Liturgy of the Word appropriate for their spiritual welfare, and suitable to their age and ability.

This can be a very valuable time for prayer and simple instruction. Children can benefit through having their own Liturgy of the Word which will help them to participate more fully in the eucharistic celebration.

I would like to take this opportunity to thank Sister Joan for all she has done in this regard throughout our diocese, helping our children towards fuller participation in the Sunday celebration of the eucharist. And I am delighted that *Welcome the Word* will now offer many more people the fruits of her experience and expertise.

+ Cormac

Cormac Murphy-O'Connor
Bishop of Arundel and Brighton

October 1989

ACKNOWLEDGEMENTS

I am very conscious of the great number of people who, in one way or another, have helped to make this book possible. I thank them all, but I cannot possibly name them all individually. I sincerely hope they recognise themselves in the organisations or groups mentioned below.

First of all I would like to record my thanks to the people of the parish of Saint Edward the Confessor, Pound Hill, Crawley. They have been a constant source of help in the work of making the Liturgy of the Word come alive for the whole parish, especially the children.

Sincere thanks, next, to the team from the Arundel and Brighton Christian Education Centre. Through their hard work, lots of typing, and not least financial support, the first diocesan editions of these liturgies were printed and circulated. If the practice of having these liturgies for children is now becoming the norm rather than the exception, it is in no small measure due to them.

I also want to thank Robert Kelly, who as editor of Geoffrey Chapman worked hard to ensure that the design and lay-out of this present edition captured the essence of the project, and honoured the centrality of the Gospel.

The Gospels in *Welcome the Word* may be simplified and/or adapted, but it was always with one eye on the text as presented in the Lectionary. This is, of course, the Jerusalem Bible translation. I gratefully acknowledge the permission granted by Darton, Longman and Todd (the publishers of the Jerusalem Bible) to do this.

Finally, there are two people I do want to mention by name, because they were particularly influential in any success my work with Liturgies of the Word for children has had: firstly, Bishop Cormac for the encouragement he has given to this work from the very beginning, and for his continuing support to stimulate the growth of simple but dignified liturgies for children throughout the diocese of Arundel and Brighton; and perhaps above all, my deepest and warmest thanks to Sister Catherine Golden, IJ, without whose vision the project might never have developed, and without whose encouragement to me personally I might never have persevered.

Sister Joan Brown, SND

To the Word

INTRODUCTION

Offering a special Liturgy of the Word for children at one or more of the Sunday Masses in a place set apart from the adult congregation, is a relatively new development, but one which has spread rapidly in the past ten years or so as its advantages and values have come to be recognised.

But why do we have it? How did it start?

In November 1973 the Sacred Congregation for Divine Worship published a document called the *Directory on Masses with Children*, which clearly spelled out the implications of, on the one hand, good liturgy and on the other, the needs of children.

The starting point is that the Church has a duty towards these children. They are baptised, and therefore they have the right to take part in the liturgy as fully as they are able:

> 'the Church is bound to be specially concerned about the welfare of children who have been baptised'; and
> 'the Church is the place where the children should receive a eucharistic education'.

However, as we all know and the *Directory* recognises,

> 'liturgical and especially eucharistic celebrations, which of their very nature have an educative value, are scarcely fully effective where children are concerned'.

We may now celebrate our liturgies in English, but the language is most often very adult, and many of the symbols will simply pass over the children's heads. Some of these symbols they will grow into, of course. As the *Directory* says,

> 'One does not have to insist that every detail of the liturgy be made comprehensible to children . . . all the same, it must surely be spiritually harmful to them to have the experience of going to church for years without ever understanding properly what is going on.'

One part of the Sunday celebration that can be adapted for children is the Liturgy of the Word:

> 'Wherever the necessary facilities are available, it is appropriate to have a special liturgy of the word and homily for the children in a separate place not too far distant from the main body of the church. Then when the eucharistic liturgy begins they can be brought back to the place where in the meantime the adults have been celebrating their own liturgy of the word.'

As I see it, providing children with a Liturgy of the Word suited to their age and adapted to their stage of development is one of the key ways of helping them to grow in faith: in becoming good, informed, spiritually formed Christians, for whom the word of the Lord has a natural but important and integral place in their daily lives.

By offering liturgy that is relevant, we will be leading children into a genuine sense of celebration: they will enjoy it, they will want to be there. Enabling children to participate fully at their own level, to be active and involved, builds up a healthy relationship between the liturgy and their daily living.

ABOUT THIS BOOK

The aim of this book is a simple one: to offer resources for celebrating with children every Sunday and major feast of the three-year cycle. There are certain principles which lie behind what is offered, which are worth making explicit.

1. One parish celebration.

Although the children may be apart fom the adults, it is in essence the same Liturgy of the Word that all are celebrating. The parish celebration should be one.

This means when the children do return at the beginning of the eucharistic celebration, any visual material, any songs or prayers they have prepared will echo what the adults have heard in the readings and homily. What is offered is always a celebration of the Liturgy of the Word. This is not Sunday school; not a creche; not playtime; the purpose is not to entertain the children. Rather, the children gather together to hear and to respond to God's word. The simplified Gospels follow those given in the Lectionary (see notes below).

2. The Gospel is central.

All the resources offered in this book follow a threefold pattern, centred on the Gospel:

- time is spent preparing to hear the Gospel;
- time is spent welcoming and proclaiming the Gospel;
- time is spent responding to the Gospel.

The book has been carefully laid out so that these three successive stages in each celebration are quite clear.

The resources this book offers are meant as suggestions. I offer a framework, based on the experience of a very successful diocesan scheme operated in Arundel and Brighton, but it is only a framework on which you should build with your own ideas and skills. Rather than follow it slavishly, use it to help you implement your own ideas; for these celebrations to work, you need to be creative, to use your imagination, to add material that is local and topical.

NOTES

Welcome the Word follows the texts given in the Lectionary. In many instances the Gospels are adapted and sometimes shortened.

For the season of Advent and Christmas, many of the celebrations in Lent and Easter, and the 'other feasts', a common Gospel text has been established for use in all three years of the lectionary cycle.

No resources are offered for Holy Thursday, Good Friday or the Easter Vigil. It is better that the children should take part in the main celebrations of these central feasts, much of whose symbolism should appeal to the children.

HOW TO USE THIS BOOK

BEFORE THE SUNDAY CELEBRATION

Several days before:
First and foremost, you should have read through the full Sunday readings. Reflect on these, and ask yourself what message the readings have for you and for your life. Look, too, at the texts of the prayers for the day.

Then turn to the relevant pages in this book. Read through and decide which of the suggestions you will use. Gather together whatever visual aids you will be using, and prepare the theme poster and the cut-out shapes.

The theme
The theme given for each celebration can be written out in large, clear letters, to make a poster or a banner. Decorate this if you like to help make it attractive, but always so that the decoration enhances and reinforces the message, rather than obscuring it.

Cut-out shapes
Throughout the book a variety of shapes are suggested. These need to be cut out beforehand. You might find it helpful to enlarge the outline drawings as models for these cut-outs. Basically, the cut-outs are intended to be work-cards for the children. They will have to write and/or draw on them, so be sure they are large enough to accommodate this. In some instances these can be cut out of coloured paper or card, and this can be especially attractive when the shapes are gathered to make a collage or frieze.

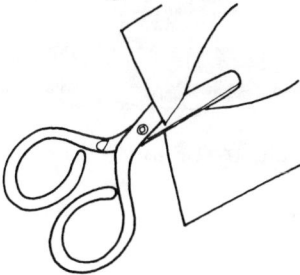

Gospel readers
If children are to take part in the proclamation of the Gospel, they should be given a copy of the text in advance to prepare it. Experience suggests giving it to them a week in advance.

ON THE DAY

The room
Prepare the room where the children are to gather for their liturgy of the word. It should be so arranged that the children appreciate that they are celebrating a liturgy, not having a religious education lesson. If tables and chairs cannot be provided, the children can use clipboards, or stiff card on the floor.

The Book of the Word

In keeping with the principle of making the Gospel central, pride of place will go to the Bible or the book of God's Word. Attention to the details of how the book looks, the privileged place it is given, will all help to build up the children's sense of respect for the word itself. So, if the book itself is not already attractive, then make a splendid cover for it, whether with card or paper or cloth, with a clear, impressive and appropriate picture (icon) on the front cover.

The altar of the Word

Prepare a table to serve as the altar of the Word. This should be the central focus for the children's attention. An ordinary table will serve well, but it should be draped with table or altar cloths. There should be a clear space for the Bible (with a stand, if necessary). Add flowers and candles to honour, show respect for God's Word. You could make the flowers and altar decoration match the liturgical season. Indeed, exploring the colours and their symbolism can be a feature of some celebrations.

Visual aids

Where the visual aids you have chosen are pictures, they can be incorporated into the theme poster/banner or displayed separately. I use a piece of stiff card, about 12" by 36" (30 cm by 90 cm), folded into three, and then covered with contact paper to which Blutack will stick. This board forms a convenient display stand for pictures and also acts as an effective background for the altar.

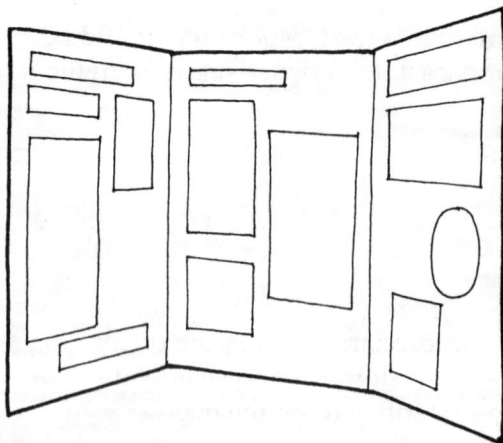

Once the children are used to the routine of what is needed, and what usually goes where, it should be possible to involve some of them in the preparation beforehand.

THE CELEBRATION

The children gather for the Sunday celebration in the main church with the rest of the parishioners. It is probably better for them to sit with their parents and families, because they will return to these places later for the eucharistic celebration. They stay in these places for the opening hymn, the entry procession, and the celebrant's greetings.

After the greeting the celebrant invites the children to come forward. He entrusts their copy of the Gospels to them, which one child will carry, and all the children leave in procession to the place where they are to celebrate their Liturgy of the Word. Note that this should be an orderly procession!

When they reach the place for their celebration, the Gospel book is enthroned on the altar prepared for it.

Settle the children, and then introduce the theme of the celebration. Be brief, and be relevant. The visual aids, the sharing activities are meant to prompt the children to contribute their experiences of the theme. Gently keep their contributions focused on the theme.

Once you think they are sufficiently well tuned into the theme, move towards the Gospel, with a simple phrase like 'Now let us listen to what Jesus tells us about . . .'. Be careful always to speak of Jesus in the present tense, which will convey to the children that we are celebrating Christ present among us, speaking to us now.

Welcome and proclaim the Gospel

Have the children stand, as a sign of respect for the word that is to be proclaimed. Light the candles. All together, say or sing the Gospel acclamation. A text is offered in the book for each celebration, but if you have an appropriate song it would be better to sing that than to say the text. The children should all make the response 'Glory to you, Lord', while signing their foreheads, lips and hearts.

The Gospel is then proclaimed. Wherever possible, give the children the honour of being ministers of the word. Choose good readers, if possible a week before they are to read so that they have time to prepare.

When the proclamation of the Gospel is complete, you can repeat the acclamation. This is especially effective if you have a sung acclamation. As a safety precaution, extinguish the candles after the proclamation of the Gospel before the discussion and activities begin.

Response to the word

The discussion and activities are meant to focus the children on how they can respond to the word that God has addressed to them today. The particular nature of the activities depends very much on the ability of the person directing the children's liturgy.

Someone musically gifted may encourage response in song. Another may feel confident with mime and drama (but note that any miming or acting out of the Gospel should be separate from the proclamation itself). Art work, banners, posters and collages may be yet another response.

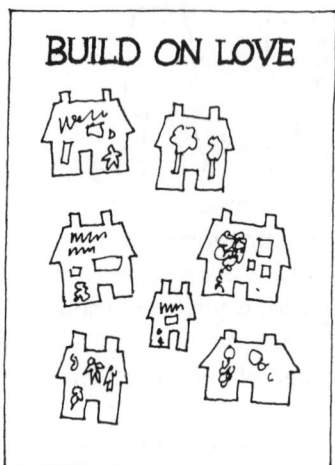

Each director should be as creative and imaginative as they can in their own given circumstances. Keep the activities as clear as possible, so that the children instinctively see the connection between what they are doing and the Gospel; and keep them as simple as possible, so that the children enjoy them.

Have a large lightweight board on which the children's work can be mounted with Blutack. This same board can carry the theme poster, and should be light enough to be taken in the procession back to the main church.

Return to the main church

You need to have a simple system established, whereby you have warning of when to close down the activities, so as to be ready to rejoin the others in the main church. This can be as simple as an usher coming in to advise you when the sermon has finished (which gives you the time it takes for the Creed and the

Prayer of the Faithful to draw the children's liturgy to a conclusion).

In some parishes acolytes and even the cross bearer come to meet the children, who then process into church, being joined by those who are bringing the gifts of bread and wine. In all events, the children process back into church (in an orderly way), one child carrying their Gospel book, two children carrying the display board. The Gospel Book should be returned to its proper place, the ambo; the display board should be placed in front of the ambo (i.e. the lectern which is reserved for the proclamation of God's Word).

Sometimes the children remain on the sanctuary, if they have prepared a special song or some prayers. The celebrant might then question the children on their work, thank them for it, or invite them to pray or sing. In this way, what the children have been doing is linked clearly and visibly with what the adults have been doing. The celebrant can then invite the children to return to their places.

After the blessing and before the dismissal, the celebrant can invite the children to collect their work from the display board and take it home with them.

Other points

Several examples are given throughout the book of how to introduce the Gloria, the Responsorial Psalm, some elements of the Creed, the Prayer of the Faithful, and other prayers. They are not included for every Sunday or feast day. However, be prepared to introduce them wherever you feel it appropriate. For example, the singing of the Gloria can flow quite naturally from the children's sharings. Similarly, depending on how the discussion has gone, you might let it lead into professions of faith or bidding prayers.

Music

The choice of music and hymns depends very much on the local situation and the abilities of those directing the children's liturgy. Do not introduce singing merely for the sake of it, but choose songs carefully that fit the theme, and offer the children a way of responding to the Gospel. Wherever possible, live music is preferable to recordings, and encourage any children who play musical instruments to help with the preparation and presentation of the music.

Discipline

As long as the children enjoy what they are doing, they will want to be present at and take part in their Liturgy of the Word, and there should be no problem with discipline. As long as the celebrations are meaningful for them, they will afford the children a sense of accomplishment. Certainly good behaviour must be expected - but it is easier for every one if this expectation arises naturally.

Certainly discipline problems are difficult in this situation if they arise. Let your approach be a positive one. Sufficient adult help is a must - a ratio of one adult to ten children is not excessive. Keep the children interested and busy. Let it be a privilege to light the candles, carry something to the altar, to be a minister of the word, to take part in a mime, etc.

BE ON THE WATCH

VISUAL AIDS

> Advent wreath, or four candles.

> Christmas tree with fairy lights.

> Mobile of sun, moon and stars.

> Either cut-out star shapes, or clock faces.

WELCOME AND PROCLAIM THE GOSPEL

Light the first Advent candle, switch on the tree lights; say/sing together:

Alleluia, alleluia!
We long for your coming,
Lord Jesus.
Alleluia!

A reading from the Good News given to us by Matthew, Mark and Luke.
Glory to you, Lord.

Jesus says,
'You will see signs, the golden sun and the silver moon and stars shining in the night sky. Let these remind you that I am coming.
Be on the watch. When the great flood came, many people were taken

DISCUSSION

What signs did Jesus say should remind us that he is coming?
- sun, moon, stars.
What signs around us remind us that Christmas is near?
- decorations, trees, cards, etc.
How can we be signs to remind people of Jesus?
- by sharing, telling the truth, praying, etc.

When would we not like Jesus to come back and see what we are doing?
- when we are being selfish, greedy, lazy, etc.
So how can we watch for Jesus and be ready to welcome him?
- by caring, sharing, praying, etc.

SHARING

Today a special time of the year begins, which is called 'Advent'. It is a time of waiting and preparing for the coming of Jesus. Encourage the children to say how they feel when waiting for something: for birthdays; for a new baby; etc. What kind of preparations do they make?
Advent is also a time for remembering. Encourage the children to share their memories of Christmas and gifts. During Advent we remember God's wonderful gifts to us. Have the children name some of the gifts given to us by God: life; parents; brothers; sisters; friends; etc. We remember especially the greatest gift of love that God gives us: Jesus, his only Son. During Advent we prepare to celebrate Christmas, to remember Jesus' being born. And we also remember his promise to come again.

by surprise.
Be on the watch. Be like Noah and his family, who were ready.
Be like faithful servants waiting for their master to come home. Stay awake. Do not let him find you sleeping.
Be on the watch and ready to welcome him when he arrives.'

This is the Gospel of the Lord.
Praise to you, Lord Jesus Christ.

ACTIVITIES

> Have the children mime short scenes illustrating not being ready; being taken by surprise.

Either:

> Give out the star shapes.
> On them have the children write or draw how they can be 'Jesus signs' in the week ahead.

Or:

> Give out blank paper and ask the children to draw how they can be a light for Jesus: e.g. a lighthouse, guiding and warning; lamp, helping people see; firelight, keeping people warm and cosy.

Or:

> Give out clock faces.
> Have the children divide them into four sections, and write how they will remember Jesus morning, afternoon, evening and bedtime.

PREPARE A WAY FOR THE LORD

VISUAL AIDS

> Advent wreath, or four candles.

> Pictures of roads: town roads, country roads, mountain roads.

> A large envelope containing the message 'PREPARE A WAY FOR THE LORD'.

> Clearway road sign

WELCOME AND PROCLAIM THE GOSPEL

Light two Advent candles.
Say/sing together:

Alleluia, alleluia!
We open our hearts
to welcome Jesus with love.
Alleluia!

The beginning of the Good News given to us by Matthew, Mark and Luke.
Glory to you, Lord.

The prophet Isaiah tells us that God says
'I promise to send my messenger to prepare a way for you.
He will call out in the wilderness, "Prepare a way for the Lord, and make straight his paths."'

DISCUSSION

What promise did God give us through Isaiah?
- that God would send us a messenger.
Who is this messenger?
- John the Baptist
What is the message he brings us from God?
- to prepare the way for the Lord.

How did the people in the Gospel prepare? What sign did they make?
- they went to the River Jordan to be baptised.
What did this sign mean?
- they wanted to start living a new life.
What did John tell them?
- someone greater was coming, who would baptise with the Holy Spirit.

SHARING

Show the envelope, and encourage the children to guess what it contains.
Lead them towards saying that it contains a message.
What might the message be?
Open the envelope and show the message.
Show the pictures, and encourage the children to talk about them: note the contrasts; talk about journeys; delays caused by bad roads; frustrations of traffic jams; etc.
Jesus wants to come into our lives. Do we make the way difficult for him, or easy?
When do we make the road difficult? By mountains of selfishness; valleys of lies; rough ways of bad temper; etc.
How can we make the way in easy? By smoothing the way with kindness, with truth, with peace, etc.

And so it was.
John the Baptist came with this message,
'Repent. Turn away from sin. Prepare a way for the Lord. Make your hearts ready to receive him. Make the path for him into your life easy.'
Many people who heard John decided to change their lives. They went to the River Jordan, where John baptised them. John told them,
'I baptise you with water, but someone is coming who will baptise you with the Spirit. He is much greater than me, so great that I'm not fit to kneel and undo his sandal straps. The baptism that he brings will change your lives completely.'

This is the Gospel of the Lord.
Praise to you, Lord Jesus Christ.

ACTIVITIES

> Give out the road signs.

> Have the children write or draw on them (or on blank paper) what it is they will do in the coming week as a sign that they are preparing for Jesus' coming.

> Have the children write a prayer asking Jesus to help them change their lives.

> Have the children mime some ways in which people change their lives.

BE HAPPY! JESUS IS COMING

VISUAL AIDS

> Advent wreath, or four candles.

> Some beautiful objects, or pictures of some.

> Pleasant music.

WELCOME AND PROCLAIM THE GOSPEL

Light three Advent candles.
Say/sing together:
Alleluia, alleluia!
Let us be ready to welcome the
Lord, for he comes.
Alleluia!
In today's Gospel there will be moments when you have to say what you think comes next. Be ready!

A reading from the Good News given to us by Matthew.
Glory to you, Lord.

Because of the way John the Baptist was asking everyone, even the King himself, to change their lives, the King had him put in prison.
But that did not stop John from hearing about the many wonderful things that Jesus was doing.
He heard how Jesus was . . .

DISCUSSION

In prison, what gift could John still use?
- hearing, he still heard about Jesus.
And what was seen and heard about Jesus?
- that he made the blind see, etc.
What gifts did Jesus bring?
- sight, hearing, life, etc.

How did the people feel about having these gifts?

- happy! To them this was Good News.

What gift do we receive?
- God the Father makes us a present of Jesus, so we should be happy, too. At Christmas we try to show our happiness by giving thanks to God for Jesus, and by giving presents to others to make them happy.

SHARING

Show the children the beautiful things; have them listen to the music.
Encourage them to share what it is they enjoy seeing, hearing.
All of these things are gifts from God: sight to see the beauty of the world, the gift of hearing.
What other things, activities do they like? Again, these are possible only because God has given us the gift of bodies, arms and legs so that we can run, jump, swim, play.
Can they use these gifts if they are alone? Some they can.
Today's Gospel tells us about someone alone, because he is locked up in prison.
Have the children guess who it is.

(What do the children think John had heard?)
So John sent some of his friends to ask Jesus a question . . .
(What do the children think the question was?)
John wanted to know 'Who are you?'
Jesus replied . . .
(How do the children think Jesus replied?)
Jesus replied,
'Go back and tell John all you have seen: that blind people see again; deaf people hear; lame people walk; lepers are healed; the dead live; the Good News is proclaimed to the poor. Anyone who believes in me is happy.'

This is the Gospel of the Lord.
Praise to you, Lord Jesus Christ.

ACTIVITIES

> On blank paper, have the children make up thank you cards to God the Father for the present he gives us, Jesus.

> Have the children draw pictures of the gifts that Jesus gave.

> Have the children mime the Gospel, including miming the various healing scenes.

> Recite this prayer together, the children repeating it phrase by phrase:
Jesus has no body now on earth,
but my body.
With my feet he walks;
with my eyes he looks with love;
with my hands he blesses;
with my tongue he speaks words
of comfort.

FILL US, LORD, WITH YOUR LOVE

VISUAL AIDS

> Advent wreath, or four candles.
> Christmas cards of Jesus and Mary.
> The individual cut-out letters of J O Y , made into a mobile.
> Either people shape cut-outs, or bell shape cut-outs.

WELCOME AND PROCLAIM THE GOSPEL

Light the four Advent candles.
Say/sing together:

Alleluia, alleluia!
We are ready to do
what God wants us to do.
Alleluia!

A reading from the Good News given to us by Luke.
Glory to you, Lord.

God sent his messenger, the angel Gabriel, to a town in Galilee called Nazareth, where Mary lived. Mary was going to be married to Joseph. 'Rejoice, Mary', the angel said, 'God has chosen you especially.'
Mary did not understand what the angel could mean, and she was

DISCUSSION

Who is the messenger we hear about in today's Gospel?
To whom did he bring the message?

What was that message?
- that Mary had been chosen by God to be the Mother of Jesus.

How did Mary feel?
- afraid, frightened.

What did Mary reply to the angel?
- 'I am ready to do . . .'

How can we make the same reply as Mary between now and Christmas?
Have the children give examples.

SHARING

Encourage the children to talk about joyful times they have experienced. So far in Advent we have heard about different messengers and the messages they brought from God. Can the children remember who the messengers were?
- Isaiah and John the Baptist.
And what was the message?
- to make ready the way of the Lord.

In today's Gospel we hear a story about another, and a rather special messenger.

frightened. The angel said, 'Mary, do not be afraid. You are going to have a baby boy. You must call him Jesus. He will be great. He will be called the Son of the Most High.'
Mary replied
'I am ready to do what God wants me to do.'

This is the Gospel of the Lord.
Praise to you, Lord Jesus Christ.

ACTIVITIES

> Divide the children up into groups of two, to practise miming the Gospel as Mary and the angel. Then have some of them mime it for the whole group.

Either:

> Give out the people shapes and have the children colour them to represent themselves. Then fasten these on a display board around a picture of Mary with the theme text 'FILL US, LORD . . .'

Or:

> Give out the bell shapes, and explain the bells ring out to show our joy at Jesus' birth.
> On the shapes have the children write or draw how they can make other people joyful.
> Have the children make a Christmas card which they can give to bring the message of love and joy to a lonely person.

JESUS IS BORN

VISUAL AIDS

> The crib.
> A Christmas tree, with lights.
> Christmas decorations and cards.
> Christmas cake, with candles.
> Christmas wrapping paper.
> An empty box, attractively gift wrapped.
> Old Christmas cards (for cutting and pasting).

WELCOME AND PROCLAIM THE GOSPEL

Say/sing together:

**Alleluia, alleluia!
Today a Saviour
has been born to us,
Jesus, our Lord.
Alleluia!**

A reading from the Good News given to us by Luke.
Glory to you, Lord.

The authorities were making a census, and everyone had to return to the town that the family belonged to. Joseph set out from Nazareth for Bethlehem, together with Mary. While they were there, the time came for her baby to be born. She gave birth to a son. She had to lay him in a

DISCUSSION

Show the children the box; get them to notice how attractive it looks. Open it, and let the children discover it is empty. Christmas without Jesus is like the empty gift box.

Have the children say who they can see in the crib scene.

Link each of the figures with an appropriate prayer that all can say together:
  lambs - Lamb of God . . .
  Mary - Hail Mary . . .
  shepherds - We believe . . .
  angels - Gloria.

SHARING

Have the children sit round the crib;
switch on the Christmas lights, light
the candles; sing a favourite carol,
e.g. *Away in a manger* or *Child in the
manger*.

manger, because there was no room
for them at the inn.
There were shepherds on the
hillside, looking after their sheep.
An angel appeared to them, and told
them,
'A Saviour has been born for you.
You will find him lying in a manger.'
Suddenly there was a great crowd of
angels, praising God and singing:
All sing:
Angels we have heard on high

ACTIVITIES

Either:
> Have the children make up crib
  collages from old Christmas cards.
Or:
> Have the children make a
  decoration to hang on the
  Christmas tree.
  Have them write or draw on it
  how they will make someone
  happy today.

WE ARE THE FAMILY OF GOD

VISUAL AIDS

> Picture of the Holy Family.
> Family photographs of the children present,
  or pictures of families.
> Pictures cut from magazines of household items.
> Pictures of people sharing, caring.
> One large house outline, and a small cut-out house for each child.

WELCOME AND PROCLAIM THE GOSPEL

Say/sing together:

**Alleluia, alleluia!
May Jesus and his Word
be at home with us.
Alleluia!**

A reading from the Good News given to us by Luke.
Glory to you, Lord.

Every year Mary, Joseph and Jesus travelled to the Temple in Jerusalem for the feast of Passover. One year, when Jesus was twelve, Joseph and Mary started to travel home, without realising that Jesus was left behind in Jerusalem. When they noticed he was not with any of

DISCUSSION

Have the children retell the Gospel story in their own words.

Invite the children to sit comfortably. Play soft music. Then invite the children to think of each member of their family in turn, and to say a prayer in their heart for that person. Then together say the family prayer of Jesus: **Our Father** . . .

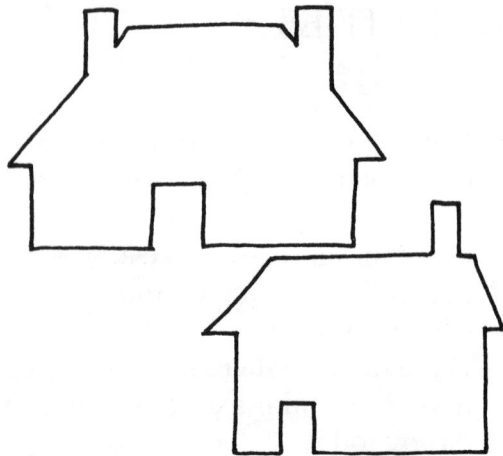

SHARING

Have the children choose from the collection of pictures cut from magazines what they think are the five most important things in a home.
Ask them what they think Jesus would have had in his home.
- family, love, care, etc.

Would he have had any of the items the children have chosen?
Have the children reconsider what they would like to have in their home, i.e. what will make it a happy place to live in?

their friends or relations, they went back to Jerusalem. Three days later they found him in the Temple, sitting among the teachers, listening to them, and asking them questions. All who heard him were astonished at how well he spoke.
When his parents found him, Mary said to Jesus,
'Why did you do this? Your father and I have been really worried about you.'

Jesus replied,
'Didn't you know that I must be busy with my Father's business?' They did not understand what he meant.
They travelled home to Nazareth. Mary remembered all these things, and Jesus grew in wisdom and in favour with both God and all who knew him.

This is the Gospel of the Lord.
Praise to you, Lord Jesus Christ.

ACTIVITIES

> Have the children draw a picture of themselves and their family having a happy day together.

> Place the children's pictures inside the large house shapes, together with the picture of the Holy Family, and the theme text WE ARE THE FAMILY OF GOD.

THE LIGHT OF THE WORLD IS COME

VISUAL AIDS

> Nativity scene: either a crib set or a picture.

> Christmas tree decorated with fairy lights, stars, candles, etc.

> A nativity picture for each child (made from old Christmas cards).

WELCOME AND PROCLAIM THE GOSPEL

Say/sing together:

Alleluia, alleluia!
Glory to you, O Christ,
light of all the world.
Alleluia!

A reading from the Good News given to us by John.
Glory to you, Lord.

In the beginning was the Word:
the Word was with God
and the Word was God.
Everything was created by the Word of God,
the Word gave life to all that is.
The Word of God gives life and light to all.

DISCUSSION

What was in the beginning?
- the Word.
Where was the Word?
- with God.
What came from the Word?
- everything that is, life and light.
What is special about this light?
- the darkness cannot put it out.
What is the power given to those who accept the Word and the light?
- the power to become children of God.
How can we reach this Word?
- because the Word became human, like us.
What do we call God's Word?
- Jesus.

SHARING

Christmas is the time when we dress the world up in beautiful decorations to show we are celebrating something very important. We are celebrating the birth of Jesus.
And a favourite kind of decoration is lights: encourage the children to give examples, e.g. fairy lights, fancy candles, fancy street lights, etc. We are celebrating that Jesus, who is the light of the world, is come.
And we use lots of words to make each other happy: what do we say? and what do we sing?

In today's Gospel we will hear Saint John tell us about Jesus coming into the world.
He will say Jesus is Word and Jesus is light. Let us listen.

The light shone in the darkness
and could not be put out.

All those who believe and accept
the Word and the light
are given great power,
the power to become children of God.
The Word of God became human, like us,
and lived among us.

We saw his glory,
the glory of the Son of God,
full of grace and truth.

This is the Gospel of the Lord.
Praise to you, Lord Jesus Christ.

ACTIVITIES

> When Jesus was born, there was a great light and the angels sang; the shepherds sang. We copy them now as we sing . . . (sing an appropriate carol with a good 'Gloria' in it!).

> The wise men travelled a long way, through many difficulties to follow the star (light) that led them to Jesus. What can we do this week that shows we are following the way of light?

> Give out the cards, and have the children write or draw what they will do to show they are people of light.

WE HAVE SEEN HIS STAR

VISUAL AIDS

> Crib, including the figures of the wise men.
> Large silver star.
> Something gold: a ring, bracelet, chain.
> Incense and thurible.
> Perfume and hand cream.
> Star shape cut-outs.

WELCOME AND PROCLAIM THE GOSPEL

Say/sing together:

**Alleluia, alleluia!
We have seen his star
and have come to worship him.
Alleluia!**

A reading from the Good News given to us by Matthew.
Glory to you, Lord.

After Jesus had been born at Bethlehem, some wise men came to Jerusalem from the east.
'Where is the new king?' they asked. 'We have seen his star and have come to worship him.' Of course, Herod the King was very worried to hear about a new king. He pretended

DISCUSSION

Have the children mime the Gospel. What were the gifts that the wise men offered Jesus?
Gold: show the golden items, and explain gold's significance as meaning wealth, power. By giving Jesus gold they were saying 'We recognise that you are worth more than all the money in the world; we recognise your power.'

Frankincense: burn some incense in the thurible and let the children smell the smoke. Explain that this was used as a sign of respect for important people. By giving this the wise men were worshipping Jesus.
Myrrh: using the perfume and cream, explain to the children that this was used especially for anointing the body after death. Giving this is a symbol of Jesus' death and resurrection.

SHARING

Gather the children round the crib, and invite them to say if they can see anything different
- the wise men;
- the star.

Have the children explain the star and the wise men in their own words.

Lead them to see that the star revealed Jesus to the wise men.

Explain that 'Epiphany' is the feast of Jesus being revealed, or shown, to the whole world.

---

he was interested in finding the child, and asked the wise men to tell him whatever they could find out, so that he too could go and worship him.

As soon as they left Herod's palace, they saw the star again. It led them to the place where Jesus was. They went in, and worshipped him. Then they offered him presents of gold, frankincense and myrrh.

An angel had warned them in a dream about King Herod, so they went back to their own country by a different way, and without telling Herod where to find Jesus.

This is the Gospel of the Lord.
Praise to you, Lord Jesus Christ.

ACTIVITIES

> Give out the star shapes, reminding the children that the star on the Christmas tree reminds us of the star that led the wise men to Jesus.

> Have the children write or draw on them:
either, how they will be wise this year, and how they will find Jesus;

or, how they will be little stars shining for Jesus so that others can find him.

WE ARE GOD'S BELOVED CHILDREN

VISUAL AIDS

> Pictures of Jesus, if possible being baptised in the Jordan by John.
> Picture of a modern day baptism.
> Candle or dove shape cut-outs.
> A large imitation candle: i.e. cardboard tube, paper to make the flame, and bright yellow felt pen.

WELCOME AND PROCLAIM THE GOSPEL

Say/sing together:

Alleluia, alleluia!
This is my Son, the beloved.
Listen to him.
Alleluia!

A reading from the Good News given to us by Matthew, Mark and Luke.
Glory to you, Lord.

Jesus came from Nazareth in Galilee to be baptised by John in the River Jordan. At first John said,
'You should be baptising me, yet you come to me!' But Jesus said
'Leave it this way for now.'
No sooner had Jesus come up out of

DISCUSSION

Where was Jesus baptised?
And who by?
What happened?
- he saw heaven opening;
- the Spirit came down on Jesus;
- a voice from heaven said . . .

The same Spirit came upon us when we were baptised.

God says the same of us, that we are his children.

Explain to the children that it was after his baptism that Jesus began his work of preaching and teaching, of spreading the Good News. We too are baptised so that we too can spread the Good News of God's love.

SHARING

Encourage the children to share their memories or experiences of baptisms.
When were they baptised?
By whom?
What name were they given?
Who are their godparents?
What promises did they make on the children's behalf?

What were the children given at baptism?
- a lighted candle.

What task were they given?
- to keep the light of faith burning brightly.

the water than he saw the heavens opening and the Spirit, like a dove, descending on him. And a voice came from heaven,
'This is my Son, the beloved.'

This is the Gospel of the Lord.
Praise to you, Lord Jesus Christ.

ACTIVITIES

Either:
> Give out the candle shapes, and either: have the children decorate them to represent their baptismal candle.
  or: have them write or draw how they will bring the light of Christ into their homes this week.

Or:
> Give out the dove shapes.
> Have the children write a prayer asking the Holy Spirit to come on them and change them into more loving and caring people.

Or:
> Make up a large imitation candle from a cardboard tube, with a large white paper flame.
> Have the children write their name on the 'flame' with the yellow pen, and have them notice how the flame becomes brighter as more names are added.

GOD MADE ME IN HIS IMAGE

VISUAL AIDS

> Lumps of clay; pots or ornaments made of clay or china.

> Picture of a potter.

> People shape cut-outs.

WELCOME AND PROCLAIM THE GOSPEL

Say/sing together:

**Praise to you, O Christ our Saviour.
We do not live on bread alone
but on every word that comes
from the mouth of God.
Praise to you, O Christ our Saviour.**

A reading from the Good News given to us by Matthew.
Glory to you, Lord.

Jesus was led by the Spirit out into the wilderness to be tempted by the devil. Jesus fasted for forty days and forty nights, after which he was hungry. The devil came and said 'If you are the Son of God, turn these stones into bread.' Jesus said 'It's more important to be hungry for

DISCUSSION

What happened to Jesus in the desert?

What were the three temptations?
- food . . . security
- power
- wealth

How, when and where are the children tempted?

36

SHARING

Encourage the children to talk about clay, and making things from clay. How do they feel about the things they make?
When the potter has finished making a nice pot, how does he feel?
- pleased and proud of what he has made
- he will not want it to be broken, damaged or spoiled in any way.

God is like the potter, we are like the pots he has made. God is proud of us, and doesn't want us to be damaged, hurt, broken or soiled in any way.

God hasn't just made us, he has made us to be like him, and to be happy with him. To do this, we follow Jesus in saying no to anything that would harm us.

God's word than to worry about bread.'
The devil then took Jesus to the top of the Temple at Jerusalem and said, 'If you are the Son of God, jump off, and God will send angels to support you.' Jesus said
'Scripture says, don't put God to the test.'
Next, taking him to a high mountain, the devil showed Jesus the whole world and said to him,

'I'll give you all this, if only you fall at my feet and worship me.' But Jesus said,
'Go away! Scripture says, worship God alone, and serve him.'

This is the Gospel of the Lord.
Praise to you, Lord Jesus Christ.

ACTIVITIES

> Have the children mime the Gospel.

> Have the children mime ways in which they are tempted, and the ways they resist temptation.

> Give out the cut-out shapes.

> On the shapes have the children write or draw how they want to grow in the image of God, the kind of person that God wants them to become.

BELIEVE GOD LOVES YOU

VISUAL AIDS

> Pictures of beautiful scenes, e.g. sunsets, etc.

WELCOME AND PROCLAIM THE GOSPEL

Say/sing together:

**Praise to you, O Christ, our Saviour.
We do not live on bread alone
but on every word that comes
from the mouth of God.
Praise to you, O Christ, our Saviour.**

A reading from the Good News given to us by Mark.
Glory to you, Lord.

The Spirit drove Jesus into the wilderness. Jesus remained there for forty days, during which he was tempted by the devil.

The angels looked after Jesus.

DISCUSSION

What happened to Jesus in the desert?
- he was tempted.

How, when and where are the children tempted?

When Jesus left the desert, what did he begin to do?

- to visit all the towns and villages.

What was the message he taught?
- believe the Good News.

What is the Good News?
- that God loves us, and wants us all to be happy with him for ever.

SHARING

Show the pictures to the children and encourage them to talk about the beauty of the world.
The world is a beautiful place. Everything God has made is good. God does not make rubbish.

God has made us, and he has made us even more wonderful than scenery. God has made us more wonderful than anything else on earth. God loves us.

Then Jesus began to visit all the towns and villages around Galilee, teaching this message:
'The time has come. God's Kingdom is close at hand. Repent, and believe the Good News.'

This is the Gospel of the Lord.
Praise to you, Lord Jesus Christ.

ACTIVITIES

> Have the children mime ways in which they are tempted, ways they resist temptation.

> Give out blank paper, and have the children write or draw:
either, ways God shows he loves them;
or, a thank you prayer to God for all the love he shows us.

JESUS GIVES US LIFE

VISUAL AIDS

> Pictures of a wilderness.

> Dead and live plants.

> Cross shape cut-outs.

WELCOME AND PROCLAIM THE GOSPEL

Say/sing together:

**Praise to you, O Christ, our Saviour.
We do not live on bread alone
but on every word that comes
from the mouth of God.
Praise to you, O Christ, our Saviour.**

A reading from the Good News given to us by Luke.
Glory to you, Lord.

Jesus set off from the banks of the River Jordan, where he had been baptised by John the Baptist. Filled with the Holy Spirit, Jesus was led into the wilderness. He was in the wilderness for forty days and forty nights, and all that time he had nothing to eat. It was during this

DISCUSSION

What happened to Jesus in the desert?

What were the three temptations?
- food . . . security;
- power;
- wealth.
How, when and where are the children tempted?

By giving into temptation we become like dried up, dead sticks instead of healthy, leafy plants. Our lives become a wilderness.

SHARING

Show the children the two sets of plants, and encourage them to discuss the difference between the dead plants with withered leaves and the live ones with fresh green leaves.

Show them how the dead branches are brittle and break if you bend them; but the green ones are supple.

We are like plants. But unless we look after ourselves, we become withered, and we could easily be broken.

time that the devil came and tempted him:
'If you are the Son of God you don't need to go hungry; just tell this stone to turn into a loaf.'
Children: **No! Don't listen!
            Don't do it, Jesus!**
Next the devil said,
'Worship me, Jesus, and I'll give you the whole world.'
Children: **No! Don't listen!
            Don't do it, Jesus!**

Then the devil said,
'Prove to me that you're the Son of God by throwing yourself from the highest tower of the Temple, and see if the angels catch you.'
Children: **No! Don't listen!
            Don't do it, Jesus !**
The devil went away and left Jesus alone.

This is the Gospel of the Lord.
Praise to you, Lord Jesus Christ.

ACTIVITIES

> Have the children mime the Gospel.

> Have the children mime ways they are tempted, ways they resist temptation.

> Give out the cut-outs.

> Have the children write or draw on them ways they want to grow in new life by being more generous, etc.

LORD, IT IS GOOD TO BE HERE

VISUAL AIDS

> Mountain scenes.

> Twigs bursting into bud.

> Cloud shape cut-outs.

WELCOME AND PROCLAIM THE GOSPEL

Say/sing together:

**Praise to you, O Christ, our Saviour.
This is my beloved son.
Listen to him.
Praise to you, O Christ, our Saviour.**

A reading from the Good News given to us by Matthew, Mark and Luke.
Glory to you, Lord.

Jesus took with him Peter, James and John, and led them up a high mountain to pray.
As Jesus prayed, he changed.
His face shone like the sun, and his clothes became as brilliant as lightning.

DISCUSSION

Where did Jesus go to pray?
Who did he take with him?
What happened?
Who appeared with Jesus?
Why did the cloud come?
- as a sign of God's presence.

The world is full of signs of God's presence; have the children give examples.

Above all, God has given us Jesus as a special sign of his presence.

What did the voice from the cloud say?
How can we listen to Jesus in the coming week?

SHARING

Encourage the children to talk about how the world is changed by sunlight.

Twigs that look dead sprout buds. Flowers open.

Have the children give examples. Everything comes alive in the warmth of spring.

Suddenly, Moses and Elijah appeared, talking to him. Peter said, 'Lord, it's good that we are here. Let us make three tents here, one for you, one for Moses and one for Elijah.'
As he spoke, a bright cloud came and covered them with its shadow, and from the cloud came a voice which said,
'This is my beloved Son.
Listen to him.'

When they heard this, Jesus' friends were terrified, and hid their faces. Jesus touched them and said 'Don't be afraid.'
And when they looked up, they saw no one - only
Jesus.

This is the Gospel of the Lord.
Praise to you, Lord Jesus Christ.

ACTIVITIES

> Have the children mime the Gospel.

> Give out the cloud shapes.

> On them, have the children write or draw:
either, ways in which they can be signs of God's love;

or, ways of following Jesus more closely.

I WILL GIVE YOU LIVING WATER

VISUAL AIDS

> Pictures of rivers, springs, waterfalls, wells, etc.

> Bucket shape cut-outs.

WELCOME AND PROCLAIM THE GOSPEL

Say/sing together:

**Praise to you, O Christ, our Saviour.
Lord, give us living water.
Praise to you, O Christ, our Saviour.**

A reading from the Good News given to us by John.
Glory to you, Lord.

Jesus was hot, tired and thirsty after his long journey when he arrived at the Samaritan town of Sychar. He sat down beside the well. While he was sitting there a Samaritan woman came along with her bucket to draw water from the well. Jesus said to her,

DISCUSSION

What did Jesus ask the woman for?

Why was the woman surprised?
- explain, as necessary, about Jews and Samaritans.

What did Jesus offer the woman?
- living water.

What does this living water bring?
- new life, eternal life.

SHARING

Talk about how life depends on water. Encourage the children to give examples, e.g. plants in the garden, for pets, crops and animals on farms. Remind the children of the new life they received in baptism when water was poured over them. Talk about the life of Jesus: has this life grown in them? how? Through love, kindness, prayer . . .

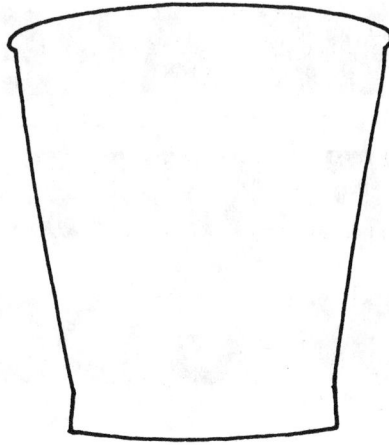

'Give me a drink.'
'What!' said the woman - she was surprised because Jews and Samaritans do not usually mix together. Jesus replied,
'If only you knew what God is offering and who it is that is asking you for a drink, you would be the one asking him for a drink, and he would give you living water. Anyone who drinks the water from this well will be thirsty again, but anyone who drinks the water that I shall give will never be thirsty again.'

This is the Gospel of the Lord.
Praise to you, Lord Jesus Christ.

ACTIVITIES

> Have the children mime the Gospel.

> Have the children mime ways of being living water:
e.g. being patient; helping at home; looking after younger brothers and sisters.

> Give out the cut-outs.

> On them, have the children write or draw:
either, ways in which their lives can be full of living water in the week ahead;
or, ways in which they can share living water with others;
or, ways in which the living water can become eternal life.

WE ARE TEMPLES OF GOD

VISUAL AIDS

> A crucifix.

> Toy animals (lambs especially), or pictures of animals.

> People shape cut-outs.

WELCOME AND PROCLAIM THE GOSPEL

Say/sing together:

**Praise to you, O Christ, our Saviour.
God loved the world so much
that he gave us his only Son.
Praise to you, O Christ, our Saviour.**

A reading from the Good News given to us by John.
Glory to you, Lord.

Just before Passover, Jesus went to the Temple in Jerusalem, where he found traders selling cattle, sheep and pigeons, and changing money. He took some cord, made a whip and chased them all out of the Temple, animals, traders and money-changers. He knocked over the tables

DISCUSSION

What was happening in the Temple?
Why was Jesus angry?
So what did he do?
What did Jesus say he could do in three days?
- rebuild the Temple.
But what did Jesus really mean?
- that he would rise from the dead.

Jesus was saying he is the Temple of God.
We too are temples of God.

What is happening in our temple?
Are we full of sacrifices?
Or full of cheating?
Encourage the children to give examples.

SHARING

Explain, as necessary, that in Jesus' time, animals and birds were offered in sacrifice at the Temple. A sacrifice is making a complete gift of something to God. Jesus offered sacrifice, but the sacrifice he offered was himself.

There was a special section in the Temple, a bit like a market, where the people could buy animals or birds for sacrifice. Some of the dealers cheated the people.

In today's Gospel we hear what happened when Jesus came along . . .

and scattered all the money. 'Get out!' Jesus said, 'You have made my Father's house into a market!'

The Jews were astonished and asked Jesus 'Why did you do this?' Jesus told them 'Knock this Temple down, and in three days I will raise it up.' 'What!' they said. 'It took forty-six years to build - how could you do it in three days?'

They did not realise that Jesus was talking about himself; that he would rise three days after being put to death. After the resurrection Jesus' friends remembered all this.

This is the Gospel of the Lord.
Praise to you, Lord Jesus Christ.

ACTIVITIES

> Have the children mime the Gospel.

> Give out the people shape cut-outs.

> On them have the children write or draw the sacrifice (the act of love) they want in their temple in the week ahead.

ANOTHER CHANCE

VISUAL AIDS

> A few healthy plants and one dying plant.

> Tree shape cut-outs.

WELCOME AND PROCLAIM THE GOSPEL

Say/sing together:

**Praise to you, O Christ, our Saviour.
Change your ways, says the Lord,
for the kingdom is near.
Praise to you, O Christ, our Saviour.**

A reading from the Good News given to us by Luke.
Glory to you, Lord.

Jesus told this story:
'A man had a fig tree in his garden. He came looking for fruit on it, but there wasn't any. So he said to the man who looked after his garden, "Look, this is the third year in a row that there has been no fruit on this tree. Cut it down, and plant

DISCUSSION

Have the children retell the story in their own words.

Why do they think the gardener wanted to try one more year?
- because of all the work he had already put in.

What do they think Jesus meant by the story?

- God the Father is the man;
- Jesus is the gardener;
- we are the trees in the garden.

If we respond to Jesus' loving care, then we will bear fruit and God our Father will be happy.

SHARING

Show the plants to the children and encourage them to talk about them.
Which is best?
Which will grow and flower?
Which one will probably die?
Which one isn't worth keeping?
What should be done with the dying plant?

Today Jesus tells a story about a tree on which no fruit was growing.

something else that will give us fruit."
"Sir", the gardener replied, "Let's try just one more year. I'll dig round it, water and feed it well. If after that there's no fruit, then we'll cut it down."'

This is the Gospel of the Lord.
Praise to you, Lord Jesus Christ.

ACTIVITIES

> Have the children mime the Gospel, with children taking it in turns to be the fig tree.
> Give out the tree shapes.
> On them have the children write or draw the fruit that they want to grow on them in the week ahead, e.g. kindness, patience.
> Say this prayer together, the children repeating it phrase by phrase:

God our Father,
you made us and you love us.
You know us by name.
You want us to produce good
**   fruit in our lives.**
Give us the strength to produce
**   the fruit you want.**
We pray too for all the people
who have already been fruitful.

HE HAS OPENED MY EYES

VISUAL AIDS

> Brightly coloured objects and pictures.

> A lamp or a lighted candle.

> Either eye shape cut-outs; or candle shape cut-outs.

WELCOME AND PROCLAIM THE GOSPEL

Say/sing together:

Praise to you, O Christ, our Saviour.
Lord, grant that we may see.
Praise to you, O Christ, our Saviour.

The children could make the blind man's response.

A reading from the Good News given to us by John.
Glory to you, Lord.

One day as Jesus was walking along the road, he saw a man who had been born blind. Jesus bent down, licked his fingers, made a muddy paste with the dust of the ground, and spread it on the man's eyes. Then he told the man,
'Go and wash in the Pool of Siloam.'

DISCUSSION

How did Jesus heal the man?

What did Jesus ask him to do?

Why did people keep asking the man what had happened to him?
- because he was so changed, he did not seem like the same person.
Jesus can do the same for us.

Once he could see, what did the man do?
- he believed in Jesus.

SHARING

Encourage the children to talk about what the world would be like without light, without colour, without eyes to see. Talk about how we need light to see clearly, the difficulty of seeing in the dark. Talk about the things the children would miss if they were blind, if it were dark all the time.

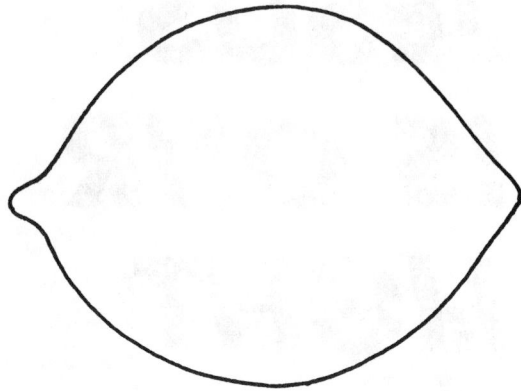

The man went, washed, and he could see. Many could not believe this was the same man, so they asked what had happened. The man said, **'Jesus made a paste, spread it on my eyes; I washed and now I can see!'** The news caused such a commotion that the priests sent for him, and they too asked what had happened: Again the man replied **'Jesus made a paste, spread it on my eyes; I washed and now I can see!'**

Many still found it hard to believe, and kept questioning the man. Again he told them, **'Jesus made a paste, spread it on my eyes; I washed, and now I can see!'** Laster, Jesus asked the man, 'Do you believe in the Son of Man?' 'Who is he?' the man replied. 'You are looking at him', Jesus said.

This is the Gospel of the Lord.
Praise to you, Lord Jesus Christ.

ACTIVITIES

> Have the children mime the Gospel.

> Give out the cut-out shapes.

> On the eye shapes, have the children write or draw how they can use their eyes to help others.

> On the candle shapes, have the children write or draw how they will keep the light of Christ burning brightly in their lives.

JESUS IS OUR LIGHT

VISUAL AIDS

> Lamp or lighted candle.

> Candle shape cut-outs.

WELCOME AND PROCLAIM THE GOSPEL

Say/sing together:

**Praise to you, O Christ, our Saviour.
Lord, fill our hearts
with the light of your Gospel.
Praise to you, O Christ, our Saviour.**

A reading from the Good News given to us by John.
Glory to you, Lord.

One of the teachers, called Nicodemus, came to Jesus by night. He believed in Jesus, and wanted to know more about him.
'Lord', he said, 'I know you are sent by God - how else could you work the signs that you do?'
Jesus replied,

DISCUSSION

Who came to see Jesus?
Why did he come at night?
- because many of the Jews were hostile to Jesus.

What did Jesus tell him?

What kind of people like the dark? Why?

And which do the children prefer, light or dark?

Remind the children of their baptism, at which they were given a candle and asked to keep the light of Christ burning brightly in their lives.

SHARING

Encourage the children to imagine and talk about what the world would be like without light and colour.
Are any of the children scared of the dark?
Do they like being out at night?

Today we have a story about a man who came to see Jesus in the night.

'I have been sent into the world to save it.
No one who believes in me will be condemned, but whoever refuses to believe will be condemned.
I am the light of the world.
Though the light has come into the world many have shown they prefer the dark.
That is because they want the dark to hide their wickedness.

It is only wicked people and liars who prefer the dark to the light.
Those who live by the truth live in the light.'

This is the Gospel of the Lord.
Praise to you, Lord Jesus Christ.

ACTIVITIES

> Give out the candle shapes.

> Have the children write or draw on them what they will do next week as a sign that the light of Christ is burning brightly in their lives.

> Have the children renew their baptismal promises:
'I promise to keep the light of Christ burning brightly in my life.'

I LOVE YOU

VISUAL AIDS

> A crucifix.

> A ring.

> Strips of paper which can be joined together to make a chain.

> Quiet, reflective music.

WELCOME AND PROCLAIM THE GOSPEL

Say/sing together:
Praise to you, O Christ, our Saviour.
Let us return to God our Father.
Praise to you, O Christ, our Saviour.

A reading from the Good News given to us by Luke.
Glory to you, Lord.

Jesus told this story:

'Once there was a rich farmer with two sons. The younger son went to his father and said,
"Father, the share of the farm that would be mine when you die, I would like it now." The father agreed, and divided the farm. A few days later the younger son left home for a far away country. As long as he had plenty of money, people wanted to be his friends, but soon it was spent and the friends left him.

DISCUSSION

Have the children retell the Gospel story in their own words.

Do they think the younger son behaved well?

How might the father have responded when the son came back home?

If one of our friends, or a brother, or a sister has hurt us, are we as kind and forgiving as the father in the story?

Show the children the ring. In the story, the father gives the son a ring. A ring has no beginning, no end. It is a symbol of the father's love, and of God's love for us.

SHARING

Have the music playing as the children are arriving, and move straight into the welcome of the Gospel.

In today's Gospel Jesus tells us a most beautiful story of love.

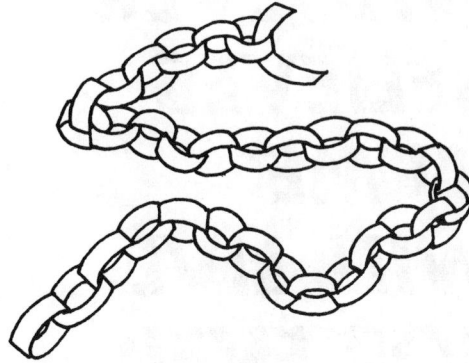

Worse, there was a famine, so soon he was starving. The only work he could find was on a farm feeding pigs.

Sitting in the pigsty one day he said, "I'm sitting here starving, while my father's servants have more food than they can eat. I'll go back home and say 'Father, I've sinned. I'm no longer worthy to be your son, but treat me as one of your servants.'" And that is what he did. While he was still a far way off, his father saw him, ran out, threw his arms around him and kissed him. The son began to say "Father, . . . " but the father called the servants.

"Hurry! Bring the best clothes for my son! A ring for his finger, and sandals for his feet! We're going to celebrate because my son has come back to life, was lost and is found.'" This is the Gospel of the Lord. **Praise to you, Lord Jesus Christ.**

ACTIVITIES

> Have the children act out the Gospel story.

> Give out the strips of paper.

> On them have the children write or draw how they will share love or forgiveness in the week ahead, and so pass God's love on to others.

> Link the strips to make a huge ring or chain of love.

WHOEVER BELIEVES IN ME WILL LIVE FOR EVER

VISUAL AIDS

> Bowl of bulbs, some just coming into flower.

> Unplanted bulbs.

> A crucifix.

> Cross shape cut-outs.

WELCOME AND PROCLAIM THE GOSPEL

Say/sing together:

**Praise to you, O Christ, our Saviour.
Lord, you are the resurrection
  and the life.
Praise to you, O Christ, our Saviour.**

A reading from the Good News given to us by John.
Glory to you, Lord.

Jesus often stayed with his friends, Martha, Mary and Lazarus in their home in the village of Bethany. So when Lazarus became very ill, his sisters sent a message to Jesus to let him know. Jesus waited two whole days before going to Bethany, and by the time he got there Lazarus had

DISCUSSION

How did Jesus feel about Lazarus?
Who were the other people in the story, and how did they feel?
What did they do . . . say?
What did Jesus do . . . say?
What do you think Lazarus felt like?
How do you think Martha and Mary felt to have their brother back?

SHARING

Invite the children to look at the unplanted bulbs. They look dead and dried up. But the power of new life is in them. Planted and watered they will grow like those in the bowl. In baptism we were given the power of new life, the life of Jesus. We were given the power to change from selfishness to love, power to be like Jesus.

In today's Gospel we hear a story about the new life that Jesus can give.

died and had been buried. Martha went to meet Jesus, and said to him, 'Lord, if you'd been here, my brother wouldn't have died.' Jesus replied, 'I am the resurrection.
Anyone who believes in me will live.'
Martha said,
'I believe, Lord.'
Then Martha and Mary took Jesus to the place where Lazarus was buried. Jesus was sad. Jesus lifted his eyes to heaven, prayed to his Father, and then said in a loud voice,
'Lazarus, come out!'
The dead man came out, with the bandages still on his hands and feet. 'Unbind him and set him free', said Jesus. Many who saw it believed in Jesus.

This is the Gospel of the Lord.
Praise to you, Lord Jesus Christ.

ACTIVITIES

> Have the children mime the Gospel.

> Give out the cross shapes.

> On them have the children write or draw what they can do to spread joy and happiness, ways of sharing the new life that Jesus has given us.

> Recite this prayer, the children repeating it phrase by phrase:
**Father in heaven,
help us to be like Jesus, your
  Son,
who loved us so much
that he died to save us.
Help us to be loving people,
so that we may bring Jesus' love
  and joy
to the whole world at Easter.**

BELIEVE IN ME AND LIVE FOR EVER

VISUAL AIDS

> Crucifix.

> Soil and flower seeds in a packet.

> Cross shape cut-outs.

WELCOME AND PROCLAIM THE GOSPEL

Say/sing together:

**Praise to you, O Christ, our Saviour.
Anyone who wants to serve the
Lord must follow him.
Praise to you, O Christ, our Saviour.**

A reading from the Good News given to us by John.
Glory to you, Lord.

Jesus was on his way to the Temple when some people came trying to see and speak to him. This is what Jesus said:
'Unless the seed falls into the ground and dies it will never be anything but a lonely seed.
But if it dies in the soil,

DISCUSSION

What did Jesus say about the seed?
- that the seed must fall and die to rise again.

And what did he say about himself?
- that he would be glorified
- that he would be lifted up.

.
What do the children think Jesus meant?

- he is talking about his death on the cross and his resurrection.

SHARING

Show the packet of seeds to the children. Open it and show them the seeds.
What use are they in the packet?
Is it better to keep them in the packet or in the dark soil?
What will happen to them in the soil?
Each seed has within it the power to become a beautiful flower.

We have the power to grow into beautiful people.
Supposing a seed wants to stay in the packet, what will happen to it? It remains dry and will never grow.
If we are selfish it is like being a seed wrapped in its packet.

Today Jesus speaks of seeds and growing.

it will grow into a plant
and produce many more seeds.
So too the time has come for me to be glorified.
My father will glorify me
and when I am lifted up
I shall draw all to myself.'

This is the Gospel of the Lord.
Praise to you, Lord Jesus Christ.

ACTIVITIES

> Give out the cross shape cut-outs.

> On them have the children write or draw the gifts they have that they want to grow.

> Say this prayer together, the children repeating it phrase by phrase:

**Father in heaven,
help us to grow more like Jesus
  every day.
He died to give us new life.
Help us to die to selfishness and
  misery,
and to be alive to love and
  happiness this Easter.**

I LOVE YOU

VISUAL AIDS

> A crucifix.
> An old treasure box containing the kind of things children like to collect: feathers; shells; buttons; etc.
> A padlock.
> Pictures of people, young, old, and different nationalities.
> A pile of stones.
> People shape cut-outs.

WELCOME AND PROCLAIM THE GOSPEL

Say/sing together:

**Praise to you, O Christ, our Saviour.
Come back to me with all your heart, says the Lord.
Praise to you, O Christ, our Saviour.**

A reading from the Good News given to us by John.
Glory to you, Lord.

Early in the morning, Jesus made his way to the Temple, where he sat down and taught the people. The scribes and Pharisees brought to him a woman who had been caught sinning.
'According to the Law given to Moses by God', they said, 'we should

DISCUSSION

Where does today's story take place?
What was Jesus doing?
Who were the people in the story?
What did they say?
What did they want to do?
Did Jesus agree with them?
What did he say to the woman?

SHARING

Show the children the old box. Encourage the children to guess its contents.
Did they expect to find treasures in an old box?
People can be like that: every person is full of treasure. But the treasure can remain locked up, hidden, because no one loves them enough to unlock it.

In today's Gospel, Jesus' love sees into a woman's heart, and helps her to change.

stone this woman to death. What do you have to say?'
Jesus replied,
'Let the person who has not sinned be the first one to throw a stone.'
After this, none of them wanted to be the first to start throwing the stones. One by one they went away, until only Jesus and the woman was left. He turned to her and said
'Go on your way, and do not sin any more.'

This is the Gospel of the Lord.
Praise to you, Lord Jesus Christ.

ACTIVITIES

> Give out the people shape cut-outs.

> On them have the children write or draw:
either, what they are most grateful for in themselves;
or, how they will share their treasures with others in the coming week.

> Say this prayer together, the children repeating it phrase by phrase:
Heavenly Father,
we are each filled with the treasure of your gifts to us.
Help us to love and care for each other,
to value your treasure in ourselves and others.

JESUS' WAY OF LOVE

VISUAL AIDS

> Palm branches.

> Set of Stations of the Cross (as detailed below) as either pictures or slides.

The Story of Jesus' Walk of Love given to us by Matthew, Mark and Luke.
Glory to you, Lord.
1. What is happening?
Pilate is asking
'What shall I do with Jesus?'
The people are shouting back,
'Crucify him!'
Pilate orders Jesus to be scourged and hands him over to be crucified.
Pray for all who are bullied.

2. What is happening?
The Roman soldiers are making a crown of thorns. They put it on Jesus. They dress him in a purple cloak. They kneel in front of him and make fun of him, saying
'Hail, King of the Jews!'
Now they dress Jesus in his own clothes. They lead him away to be crucified.
Pray for those who have to accept hard things.

5. What is happening?
They have reached a place called Golgotha. The soldiers set about crucifying Jesus. They have stripped off his clothes. They are nailing Jesus to the cross. They gamble to see who would have Jesus' clothes.
Pray for those who are poor, who have nothing of their own.

6. What is happening?
Jesus is nailed on the cross. The passers-by are making fun of him. They say,
'If he really is the King, why can't he get down off the cross?'
The chief priests and the Pharisees join in,
'He saved others, now let him save himself!'
Pray for the helpless and the handicapped.

SHARING

The children should have taken part in the procession of palms, only coming to their own place for the Liturgy of the Word.

Begin by talking about the palms, the procession and what they mean.

Lead on to explaining that today is Passion Sunday, when we remember how much Jesus loves us; we remember in particular the way in which he showed that love.
Today we are going to follow him on that walk of love.
Say/sing together:
Praise to you, O Christ, our Saviour.
Jesus gave himself for us,
even accepting death.
Praise to you, O Christ our Saviour.

---

3. What is happening?
Jesus is carrying his cross to Calvary. He is very weak. The soldiers grab a man from the crowd. His name is Simon, and he has just come to Jerusalem from Cyrene. The soldiers make Simon help Jesus to carry the cross.
Pray for all helpers; especially those who have no choice about helping.

4. What is happening?
The women are crying. They have been following Jesus. Jesus turns to them and says,
'Don't cry for me. Cry instead for yourselves and your children.
If they do this to me, what might they do to you?'
Pray for all who are sad; for all we meet as we make our way through life.

---

7. What is happening?
Though it is still afternoon, the whole land is covered in darkness. Jesus calls out loudly the words of the psalm,
'My God, my God, why have you deserted me?'
With a loud cry, Jesus dies.
Have the children kneel and pray silently.

8. What is happening?
It is evening now. Jesus' friends take Jesus' body from the cross, wrap it in a clean shroud, and carry it to a new tomb cut in the rock. They put Jesus in the tomb. They roll a large stone across the entrance of the tomb, and go away.
Pray with thanks for Jesus, who has given himself to us completely; pray that we will love and give as Jesus has.

ALLELUIA! JESUS IS RISEN! ALLELUIA!

VISUAL AIDS

> Resurrection pictures.
> Materials to make a Resurrection cross (i.e. no crucified figure, and either white cloth draped over it, or decorate it with flowers).
> Easter eggs and cards.
> Resurrection garden.
> Candle shape cut-outs.

WELCOME AND PROCLAIM THE GOSPEL

Say/sing together:

**Alleluia, alleluia!
Christ is risen.
let us celebrate!
Alleluia!**

A reading from the Good News given to us by John.
Glory to you, Lord.

On the first day of the week, early in the morning while it was still dark, Mary Magdalen went to Jesus' tomb. When she saw that the stone had been rolled away from the entrance she went running to Peter and John to say,
'Someone's taken Jesus' body away!'

DISCUSSION

Who are the people mentioned in today's Gospel?
- John, Peter, Mary Magdalen, Jesus.

What happens?

What did they see?

What happens to Mary Magdalen?

ACTIVITIES

> Have the children mime the Gospel.

> Have the children complete or work out the following, in either words or mime:
'If I had seen the empty tomb I would have . . .'

SHARING

Encourage the children to talk about
what Easter means to them.
It is the greatest, the most important
celebration of the friends of Jesus.
Why? Because we celebrate that
Jesus who died, is alive again, and
can never die again.
To celebrate the resurrection, sing
together 'Alleluia!'

They all went back to the tomb
together. They saw that the linen
cloth in which Jesus' body had been
wrapped were all still there. Mary
stayed outside the tomb, crying.
Someone else came up behind her.
Mary thought it was the gardener.
'Why are you crying?' he asked.
Mary replied,
'They have taken my Lord away, and
I don't know where they have put
him. Do you know where he is?'

The stranger said,
'Mary!' and at once Mary knew that
this was Jesus. He told her to go and
tell the other disciples that she had
seen him, and all the things he had
said to her.

This is the Gospel of the Lord.
Praise to you, Lord Jesus Christ.

Either:
> Give out blank paper/card and
have the children make an Easter
card with an Easter message.

Or:
> Give out the candle shapes and
have the children decorate them
to make them into Easter candles.

> Make a Resurrection cross: i.e.
decorate a plain cross with
flowers, ribbons, etc. to celebrate
the triumph of Jesus over death.

JESUS IS RISEN

VISUAL AIDS

> A cardboard or wooden cross covered in gold paper.

> Spring flowers.

> Eggs, chickens (or pictures).

> Flower and egg shape cut-outs.

WELCOME AND PROCLAIM THE GOSPEL

Say/sing together:

**Alleluia, alleluia!
Happy are those
who believe in Jesus.
Alleluia!**

A reading from the Good News given to us by John.
Glory to you, Lord.

On the Sunday evening after Jesus had died on the cross, all his friends were scared and hiding in the house with the doors and windows shut tight. Suddenly, Jesus was there, standing among them.
'Peace be with you' he said, and showed them his hands and his side.

DISCUSSION

What is the first thing Jesus says each time?
- peace: Jesus comes to bring us the new life of peace.

What happens to Thomas?
- he changes; from doubt to belief. The risen Jesus comes to change everyone for the better.

Encourage the children to give examples of other ways people could change.
- from selfish to generous;
- bad temper to good temper;
- dishonest to honest.

SHARING

Show the children the eggs, chickens and flowers. Encourage them to give other examples of signs of new life.

Show them the cross and explain it is golden, because it is a glorious cross. It is where Jesus conquered death, to rise to give us new life. The cross is the sign of Jesus' victory.

Praise God for Jesus' victory by singing or saying a Gloria.

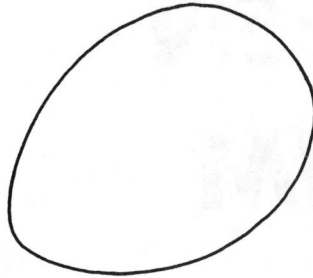

Thomas was out when Jesus came, so when the others told him they had seen Jesus, he refused to believe it. 'Unless I see for myself, and put my fingers in the holes in his hands, and my hand in the hole in his side, I will not believe.' A week later, they were all in the house again, including Thomas, when once more Jesus stood among them.
'Peace be with you' he said. Then he turned to Thomas:

'Thomas, here are my hands; come, put your fingers in the holes. See my side; come, put your hand in. Doubt no longer, but believe.' Thomas said 'My Lord and my God.'
Jesus said
'You believe because you can see me. Happy are those who have not yet seen and yet believe.'

This is the Gospel of the Lord.
Praise to you, Lord Jesus Christ.

ACTIVITIES

> Have the children mime the Gospel story.
> Decorate the cross with the flowers.
> Give out the cut-out shapes, and have the children write or draw on them what way they want Jesus to help them change in the next week.

> Recite this prayer together, the children repeating it, line by line:
God our Father,
source of life and goodness,
full of love and beauty.
You share everything with us,
even your only Son, Jesus.
Father, we thank and praise you
for the new life
which Jesus gives us
by his death and resurrection.

WE HAVE SEEN HIM

VISUAL AIDS

> Pictures of Jesus.

> Easter candle.

> Bread.

> Heart shape cut-outs.

> Quiet, sad, mood music.

PROCLAIM THE GOSPEL

A reading from the Good News given to us by Luke.
Glory to you, Lord.

Two of Jesus' friends were on their way to a village called Emmaus, talking about all that had happened over the past few days.
Have the children discuss what happened over those days, especially Good Friday.

While they were talking someone came along and joined them. It was Jesus, but they did not recognise him. 'What are you talking about?' he asked. Sadly, they replied 'You must be the only person in Jerusalem who doesn't know what's been happening here. How Jesus of Nazareth was crucified. We had hoped he would be the one to set us free. Worst still, now it seems his tomb is empty. Some of the women say angels told

DISCUSSION AND ACTIVITIES

> Divide the children into three groups:
  1. Jesus' friends in the Upper Room
  2. The two friends and Jesus
  3. Innkeeper, servants and customers in the inn.
> Mime the Gospel:

1. The Upper Room group listen as Peter, John and the women describe the empty tomb (Easter Sunday Gospel).
2. The two friends set out for Emmaus; the stranger joins them. Narrate what happens.
3. Arrival at the inn; welcome by innkeeper; served by servants; the meal; Jesus breaks bread; friends recognise him; dash back to Jerusalem.

SHARING

Use this time to set the mood for today's Gospel.

Have the children sit quietly. Invite them to imagine that they are Jesus' friends, all gathered together in the Upper Room on the first Easter Sunday.

They have heard that the body of Jesus is missing from the tomb.

They are upset, frightened.

Use the music to help establish the mood.

Let the children remain seated in this way for the proclamation of the Gospel.

them Jesus is risen, but none of our friends have seen anything of him.' Then Jesus said,

'You foolish people! Why can't you see this is what the prophets said would happen, that the Christ would suffer and so enter into his glory!' And going through all the scriptures, Jesus explained everything that was about himself. They reached Emmaus in the evening, and invited Jesus to join them at the inn for a meal. When they sat at the table, Jesus took the bread, blessed it, broke it, and shared it with them. Immediately they recognised that it was Jesus, but he vanished from their sight.

'Didn't our hearts burn within us as he talked to us on the road' they said to each other. They went straight back to Jerusalem to tell the others. This is the Gospel of the Lord.
Praise to you, Lord Jesus Christ.

4. Back to Upper Room; excitement and happiness as they exchange stories of having seen Jesus.

> Give out the cut-out shapes.

> Have the children write or draw on them how they will spread the happiness of Jesus in the week ahead.

PEACE BE WITH YOU

VISUAL AIDS

> Pictures of Jesus.

> Pictures of fish.

> Book shape cut-outs.

WELCOME AND PROCLAIM THE GOSPEL

Say/sing together:

**Alleluia, alleluia!
Lord Jesus, explain to us
    the Word of God.
Alleluia!**

A reading from the Good News given to us by Luke.
Glory to you, Lord.

Jesus' friends were gathered in the Upper Room, talking how Jesus had been seen on the road to Emmaus, and by Simon.
Suddenly, Jesus stood among them. They were frightened, because they thought it was a ghost. Jesus said 'Peace be with you! Why are you

DISCUSSION

Where were Jesus' friends?
When Jesus first appeared who did they think it was?
- a ghost.
What did Jesus say to them?
What did he ask them for?
What did they give him to eat?
What did Jesus tell them was written in the scriptures?

What did he say he would bring to the world?
How did his friends feel?
- happy, overjoyed.
What did Jesus say they were to be?
- witnesses.

SHARING

Jesus is risen from the dead.

What does this mean?
- that he is alive.

What can living people do?
- walk, talk, eat, etc.

Listen now to how Jesus' friends found him after the resurrection.

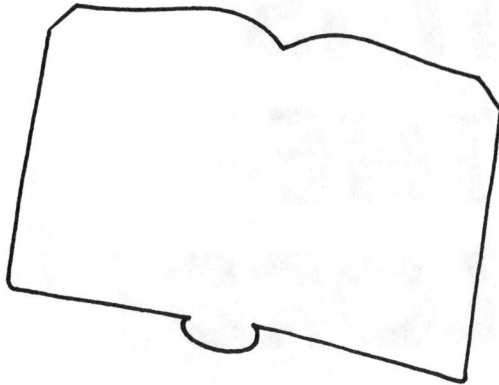

afraid? It's me - touch me and see for yourselves!'
His friends were so overjoyed they didn't know what to say. Then Jesus said to them,
'Have you got anything to eat?'
They gave him some cooked fish and he ate it. Then he explained to them what everything in the scriptures meant about the Christ having to suffer and die - but on the third day he would rise from the dead. And

that he would bring peace to the whole world. Then Jesus said 'You are all witnesses to this.'

This is the Gospel of the Lord.
Praise to you, Lord Jesus Christ.

ACTIVITIES

> Have the children act out or mime the Gospel.

> Give out the cut-outs.

> On them, have the children write or draw:
either, how they will witness to Jesus in the coming week;

or, how they will share and spread Jesus' peace.

IT IS THE LORD!

VISUAL AIDS

> Pictures of seashores, boats.

> Seashells, fishing nets, fish.

> Fish shape cut-outs.

WELCOME AND PROCLAIM THE GOSPEL

Say/sing together:

Alleluia, alleluia!
Jesus, you are the Lord.
Alleluia!

A reading from the Good News given to us by John.
Glory to you, Lord.

One evening Peter said
'I'm going fishing.' The others said
'We'll come with you.'
They set out onto the lake and fished all night, but by morning they hadn't caught a single fish. Then they heard a man calling to them from the shore, 'Have you caught anything?'

DISCUSSION

What did Jesus' friends decide to do?
Did they catch any fish at first?
- no.

When did they catch fish?
- after meeting Jesus.
Where was Jesus?
What was he doing?
Who recognised him first?

Who swam ashore?

How does the story end?
- sharing breakfast of bread and fish together.

SHARING

Show the pictures and encourage the children to share happy memories of times at the seaside: sunshine, sea, sandcastles, rockpools, picnics, etc.

In today's story we hear about a picnic at the lakeside.

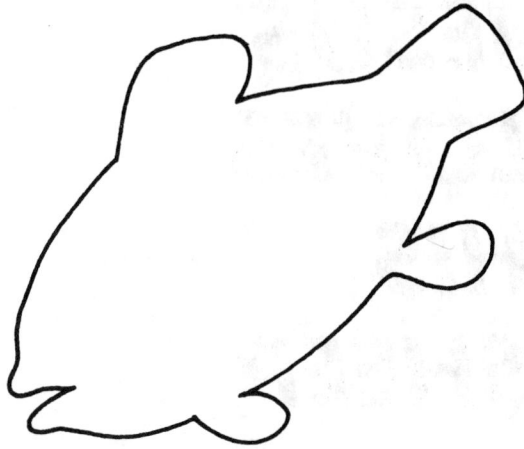

'Not a single fish!' they shouted back. 'Throw your nets out to starboard and you'll find something' he called back.
They did as he said, dropped their nets, and soon they were so full of fish that they could hardly pull them in. As they got near the shore John recognised the man on the shore and said
'It's Jesus!' Immediately Peter put his cloak on and jumped into the sea.

The others followed in the boat, dragging the nets full of fishes. When they reached Jesus they saw he had a fire ready with some bread. 'Bring me some of the fish you've just caught' said Jesus. They did, and all had breakfast of bread and fish together.

This is the Gospel of the Lord.
Praise to you, Lord Jesus Christ.

ACTIVITIES

> Either have the children mime the Gospel.

> Or divide the children into groups, give them blank paper and have them illustrate part of the story. The pictures will be put together to make a frieze or cartoon strip telling the story.

> Give out the cut-out shapes.

> Have the children write or draw on them what they can share with someone in the week ahead.

> Gather the 'fish' and attach them to the net.

73

JESUS LOVES HIS SHEEP

VISUAL AIDS

> Pictures of sheep, shepherds.

> Sheep shape cut-outs.

WELCOME AND PROCLAIM THE GOSPEL

Say/sing together:

Alleluia, alleluia!
I am the good shepherd, says Jesus.
I know my sheep and
they know me.
Alleluia!

A reading from the Good News given to us by John.
Glory to you, Lord.

Jesus says,
'I am the good shepherd.
I know my sheep and they know me.
They follow me
because they know my voice.
The shepherd comes in to the sheepfold by the gate,
but the thief who comes to kill and

DISCUSSION

Encourage the children to describe in their own words what Jesus says about caring for sheep.

Jesus wants us to follow him, like sheep follow the shepherd. Have the children give examples of following Jesus.

Some people follow Jesus by becoming priests, sisters, missionaries.

SHARING

Encourage the children to share what they know about sheep and shepherds.
A good shepherd knows each of his sheep by name.

Have the children talk about how they got their names: who chose them?

Have the children say who has called them by name in the past week, and why.

Today's Gospel story is about a special shepherd and special sheep.

destroy
sneaks in through a hole in the wall.
If a wolf attacks my sheep,
I will not run away and leave them.
I love my sheep,
and I will protect them with my life.'

This is the Gospel of the Lord.
Praise to you, Lord Jesus Christ.

ACTIVITIES

> Give out the cut-out shapes and have the children write or draw how they will respond when their name is called in the week ahead, e.g. at bed-time, at meals, etc.
> Game:
    - form a circle;
    - choose one child to be Jesus; three or four to be thieves outside the circle; two to be the gateway; some children to be sheep within the circle; the rest form the circle;
    - Jesus and the 'thieves' take turns to call 'sheep' from the circle by name. The 'sheep' have to listen carefully and only leave when 'Jesus' calls.
> Recite this prayer together:
    Lord Jesus, our loving shepherd,
    help us to hear you always
    and to say 'yes'
    when you call our names.

WELCOME!

VISUAL AIDS

> Pictures of houses and families at home.

> Several card sets of the individual letters of W E L C O M E .

> House shape cut-outs.

WELCOME AND PROCLAIM THE GOSPEL

Say/sing together:

**Alleluia, alleluia!
Jesus will show us
the way to the Father.
Alleluia!**

A reading from the Good News given to us by John.
Glory to you, Lord.

Jesus says,
'My friends,
never be upset in your hearts.
Keep on trusting in God and in me.
In my Father's house there is room for everyone,
and I am going to get a place ready for you.

DISCUSSION

Jesus says we never need be upset in our hearts: why?

What does Jesus promise that he is doing for us?

What does he ask us to do in return for the welcome he is preparing for us?
- trust him.

We have a prayer of trust in God the Father, God the Son and God the Holy Spirit; it is called the Creed.
Make up a simple Creed together, saying:
'I trust God the Father
because . . . (he created me);
I trust in Jesus, his Son, because . . .
(he died to save me);
I trust in the Holy Spirit, who . . .
(makes me a child of God).

SHARING

Give out the letter cards and challenge the children to discover the word they make.

Encourage the children to talk about ways of making people welcome. Who needs welcoming?
- children starting new school, new class; new brothers and sisters, etc. Who welcomes us?
- friends, relations, etc, when we go visiting, etc.

For all people who welcome us say or sing a Gloria - which was the song the angels used to greet the birth of Jesus.

In today's Gospel Jesus tells us about the welcome he is preparing for us in his Father's house.

When your place is ready I myself will come for you and take you to my Father's house.
Then you and I will live together forever.

Trust in me and
you will be welcome
in my Father's house for ever.'

This is the Gospel of the Lord.
Praise to you, Lord Jesus Christ.

ACTIVITIES

> Give out the house shapes.

> On them have the children write or draw:
either, a way in which they will make someone feel welcome in the next week;
or, the person they will welcome in the week ahead.

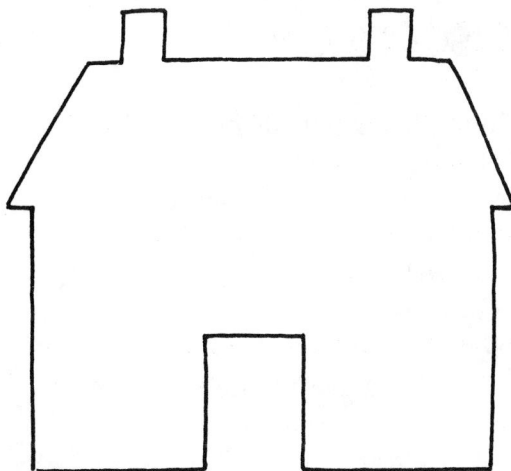

JESUS IS THE VINE

VISUAL AIDS

> Picture of a vine.
> Bunch of grapes.
> Plant, with some dead leaves/branches.
> Scissors/secateurs.
> Bunch of grape shape cut-outs.
> Large vine drawn on card.

WELCOME AND PROCLAIM THE GOSPEL

Say/sing together:

**Alleluia, alleluia!
Those who bear fruit
give glory to the Father.
Alleluia!**

A reading from the Good News given to us by John.
Glory to you, Lord.

Jesus says,
'I am the true vine,
and my Father is the vinedresser.
On the vine there are many branches.
Some are full of beautiful fruit
but some have none.
Any branch that bears no fruit
my Father cuts away.

DISCUSSION

Today Jesus tells us he is . . .?
- the vine.
Who are the branches of the vine?
- we are.
Who looks after this vine?
- God the Father.
How?
- by cutting away bad branches, branches without fruit.

Are there any unwanted branches in our lives?
Things which weaken us and prevent us bearing good fruit?
- selfishness? bad temper? etc.

What are the good fruits we should show instead?
- being thoughtful, patient, caring.

SHARING

Encourage the children to talk about looking after flowers, plants.

Give examples of how trees need pruning, grass needs cutting.

Demonstrate with the plant, cutting away the dead or dying leaves and branches to make way for the healthy ones.

At the end of the growing season the old branches are cut away to make way for the new ones for next year.

In today's Gospel Jesus talks about one particular plant as an example.

Listen carefully, because there will be questions afterwards!

A branch cut off from the vine dies, and is no good anymore.
Only branches on the vine can produce fruit.
So remain in me and you will bear much fruit
to the glory of my Father.'

This is the Gospel of the Lord.
Praise to you, Lord Jesus Christ.

ACTIVITIES

> Give out the cut-out shapes.

> On them have the children write or draw:
either, the way they will bear good fruit next week;
or, a prayer asking Jesus to help them be healthy fruitful branches.

> Gather the 'bunches' and attach them to the vine.

> Explain how the branches of a vine twist and intermingle.
Have the children all join hands to make a vine;
have them centre on the table of the Word so that 'Jesus' is the main stem, and the children are the branches.

I LOVE YOU

VISUAL AIDS

> Pictures of people, as varied as possible (different nationalities, sizes, shapes, etc.).

> Heart shape cut-outs.

WELCOME AND PROCLAIM THE GOSPEL

Say/sing together:

**Alleluia, alleluia!
This is my command,
that you love one another
as I love you.
Alleluia!**

A reading from the Good News given to us by John.
Glory to you, Lord.

Jesus says,
'My children,
I have something special to ask that you do above all else.
I want you to love one another
as I love you.
By the love that you have for one another

DISCUSSION

What is the one thing above all Jesus asks us to do?
- to love others as he loved us.

How did Jesus show his love for us?
- by giving his life for us.

Do the children know of anyone else who has done this?

What other things do people do to show their love?
- get married and give their lives to one another
- mothers and fathers give up things for their children.

Encourage the children to offer examples.

SHARING

Encourage the children to talk about how different people can be:
- some are fat; some are thin
- some are tall; some are short
- some are brown, yellow, black
- some have two arms, some have none.

But each of us is made by God.
Each of us is loved, as we are, by God.

And each of us is asked by God to love the fat, the thin, etc.

As a sign of how we shall love others, let us offer each other a sign of peace.
(Sing a suitable song, if possible.)

In today's Gospel we hear Jesus tell us what, above all, he wants us to do.

everyone will know that you are my friends.
People will say
"We know you're a friend of Jesus, because you are just like him."'

This is the Gospel of the Lord.
Praise to you, Lord Jesus Christ.

ACTIVITIES

> Have the children mime the ways that people show their love.

> Give out the cut-out shapes.

> On them have them write or draw something they will give up in the week ahead to show love, e.g. a TV programme, a game, some of their time, etc.

A GIFT FROM JESUS

VISUAL AIDS

> Pictures of friends enjoying life together.

> Picture of Jesus with people.

> Either heart shape cut-outs, and a 'caring tree' on which to hang the hearts (e.g. a branch upright in an appropriate container).

WELCOME AND PROCLAIM THE GOSPEL

Say/sing together:

**Alleluia, alleluia!
Anyone who loves God
listens to his Word.
Alleluia!**

A reading from the Good News given to us by John.
Glory to you, Lord.

Jesus says,
'If you love me
you will do what I have taught you.
I will ask my Father to send you
the Holy Spirit
to be your friend for ever.
He will help you remember
all I have told you.

DISCUSSION

Did the children notice what it was that Jesus said twice?
- that if we love him, we will do what he has taught us.

What does he promise us if we do this?
- that he will not leave us;
- that he will send us his Spirit;
- that his Father will love us;
- that he will give us his peace.

What else is a sign of being Jesus' friends?
- that we have to carry on Jesus' work in the world.

What is this work?
- spreading the good news of love and peace.

> Or attractive gift wrapped packets but with dull contents e.g. an old sock, a piece of used soap, etc.

> Large gift tag marked 'A GIFT FROM JESUS'.

> Small gift tags.

> On individual cards, the letters P E A C E .

SHARING

Give out the letter cards, and have the children discover the word.

Jesus promises his Spirit and the gift of peace to all who are his friends.

But who are his friends? Jesus will tell us clearly twice in today's Gospel.

I leave you my peace.
I will not leave you,
but I will come back to you
If you are my friends you would be glad to know I'm returning to my Father.
As the Father loved me
so I have loved you.
To show that you love me
do all I have taught you.
And when you love me,
my Father loves you.

Love one another
as I have loved you.
The proof of a true friend is
their readiness to die for you.
You didn't choose me.
I chose you.
I am sending you out
to carry on the work
the Father gave me.'

This is the Gospel of the Lord.
Praise to you, Lord Jesus Christ.

ACTIVITIES

Either:
> Give out the heart shapes.
> On them have the children write or draw how it is they will spread Jesus' love and peace by a special act of caring in the week ahead, e.g. by promising to visit a lonely person.
> Fasten the completed hearts to the branch to make a 'caring tree'.

Or:
> Give out the gift tags.
> On one side have the children write 'A gift from . . .(their own name)'.
> On the other side, have them write or draw a way they will help share Jesus' gift of peace with someone in the coming week.
> Gather the children's tags on to a display around the larger tag 'A gift from Jesus'.

SPREAD THE GOOD NEWS

VISUAL AIDS

> Decorated Easter candle.

> Picture of the risen Jesus.

> One small candle or votive light for each child.

> Candle shape cut-outs.

WELCOME AND PROCLAIM THE GOSPEL

Say/sing together:

Alleluia, alleluia!
I am with you always,
even to the end of time.
Alleluia!

A reading from the Good News given to us by Matthew and Mark. **Glory to you, Lord.**

Jesus had arranged to meet his eleven friends on a mountain in Galilee. Jesus came up and said to them:
'Go out to the whole world; proclaim the Good News to all creation. Make all people children of God, baptising them in the name of the Father and

DISCUSSION

What happens in today's story?
- Jesus returns to his Father.
Now, as a sign that he has returned, we put out the big Easter candle - but not your little candles.

What task did Jesus give his friends?
- to carry on Jesus' work of spreading the Good News.

That is why we don't put out our little candles. To show that we are Jesus' friends, and want to carry on his work, we keep our little candles burning. They show that we want to be the light of the world.

Do we have to keep our candles burning until Jesus comes again? Not the little candles, but we have to keep our hearts burning with love for Jesus and his work.

SHARING

In today's feast we celebrate Jesus' return to his Father.
Show them the Easter candle (which should be lit) and explain how it has been lit since Holy Saturday night as a sign that the risen Jesus is with us. Now, after today's Gospel, as a sign that Jesus returns to his Father, we put the candle out.

Though Jesus may be gone, his work has to continue. It is Jesus' friends who have to continue Jesus' work in the world.

Now, let us each light our candle, and listen to Jesus' farewell message; listen carefully to what he asks us to do.

of the Son and of the Holy Spirit. Teach them to do all the things I have told you. Know that I am with you always, yes even to the end of time.'
After Jesus had spoken to them he was taken up into heaven.

This is the Gospel of the Lord.
Praise to you, Lord Jesus Christ.

ACTIVITIES

> Extinguish the little candles.

Either:

> Give out the candle shapes.

> On them have the children write or draw:
either, how they will be lights of Christ in the week ahead;

or, how they will spread the Good News, and show they are Jesus' friends.

or:
> Give out a large piece of paper, and have the children draw round their feet. Then on the footprints, have them write how they are ready to set out to spread Jesus' Good News of love, forgiveness, peace, etc.

GLORY BE TO THE FATHER

VISUAL AIDS

> Pictures of Jesus.

> Pictures of people praying, e.g. at Lourdes.

> Hand shape cut-outs.

> Quiet, reflective music.

WELCOME AND PROCLAIM THE GOSPEL

Say/sing together:

Alleluia, alleluia!
I will not leave you, says the Lord,
I will come to be with you.
Alleluia!

A reading from the Good News given to us by John.
Glory to you, Lord.

Looking to heaven, Jesus prayed to his Father:
'Father, give me your glory now.
I have given glory to you on earth.
I have finished the work
you sent me to do.
I have made your name known to those you gave to me.

DISCUSSION

Who is Jesus praying for in today's Gospel?
- for us.
What is it that Jesus prays for, for us?
- that we'll always be one with him.
What does it mean to be with Jesus for ever?
When does Jesus share his glory with us? When do we become a member of God's family?

- in baptism.

Have the children sit quietly, thinking about Jesus praying for them. Quiet music should help the mood.

Lead them into praying for others, e.g. in bidding prayers, or possibly the Lord's Prayer with actions.

SHARING

Encourage the children to talk about prayer.
When do they pray?
How do they pray?
Why do they pray?
When do people pray for others?

Today we shall pray together a poem of thanksgiving.

Response
My soul, give thanks to the Lord.

Arms stretched high
My soul give thanks to the Lord,
Cross arms over breast, bow down
all my being bless his holy name,
Move arms out in wide circle
and never forget all his blessings.
Response

Protect my friends from evil,
keep them close to you.
I pray for them now,
because I am coming to you
but they have to remain in the world.
I have passed on your word to them.
As you sent me into the world,
I send them into the world.
I pray for all those in the world
who will believe in me
now and forever.
I pray that they will all be one family,
just as you and I are.
I have shared my glory with them,
so that the world might know
it is you who sent me.'

This is the Gospel of the Lord.
Praise to you, Lord Jesus Christ.

ACTIVITIES

> Give out the hand shapes.

> Invite the children to think of a person that they want to pray for. Then, on the shapes, have the children:
either, write a prayer for the person they have thought of;
or, draw a picture of that person.

COME, HOLY SPIRIT

VISUAL AIDS

> Pictures of Jesus.
> Birthday cake and birthday cards.
> Seven candles.
> Seven gift-wrapped packages; inside, cards marked with one of the gifts of the Spirit (joy; love; patience; kindness; understanding; reverence; courage).
> Dove or flame shape cut-outs.

WELCOME AND PROCLAIM THE WORD OF THE LORD

Say/sing together:

**Alleluia, alleluia!
Come, Holy Spirit, fill our hearts with the fire of your love.
Alleluia!**

A reading from the Story of the Early Church given to us by Luke.

It was Pentecost day, and all Jesus' friends were gathered in the room where they had met for the Last Supper. Suddenly they heard what sounded like a powerful wind from heaven, and it seemed the whole house was full of its noise. Something appeared to them that seemed like tongues of fire. These

DISCUSSION

Recall with the children that before he returned to his Father, Jesus promised to send the Holy Spirit.

The Holy Spirit gives us the gifts we need to carry on Jesus' work, the gifts we need to be like Jesus.

Open the gift packets, and take out the 'gifts' printed on the cards.

Together, talk of examples of people who use one or more of these gifts.

SHARING

Today is the birthday of the Church. On our birthdays we receive cards and gifts. Often the gifts help us do something, e.g. paint, draw, read, etc.
The birthday of the Church is a celebration for us too, and so we receive special messages and gifts from God.

Today we listen to a story, not from the Gospel, but from the second book that Luke gave us, which is the Story of the Early Church.

separated and came to rest on the heads of each one of them. They were all filled with the Holy Spirit. They began to preach the Good News.

Jerusalem was full of people from all round the world who had come for the feast. But amazingly, all of these foreigners not only heard Jesus' friends, but could understand them. They said,

'We hear them preaching in our own language about the marvels of God.'

This is the Word of the Lord.
Thanks be to God.

ACTIVITIES

> Have the children take it in turns to mime a 'gift'; the rest have to guess which 'gift' is being mimed.

> Give out the cut-outs.

Either:
> Have the children make a badge with them of the gift they would like the Holy Spirit to send them.

Or:
> Have the children write on them the Alleluia verse:
> **Come, Holy Spirit,**
> **fill our hearts**
> **with the fire of your love.**

JESUS IS THE CHOSEN ONE OF GOD

VISUAL AIDS

> Picture of Jesus.

> Pictures of people doing everyday things.

> Dove shape cut-outs.

WELCOME AND PROCLAIM THE GOSPEL

Say/sing together:

Alleluia, alleluia!
Here is the Lamb of God
who takes away
the sin of the world.
Alleluia, alleluia!

Today some of the words of the Gospel will be left out deliberately; listen carefully and fill them in.

The words to be omitted during the proclamation are presented in brackets.

DISCUSSION

What does John call himself?
- a witness
- a person who sees something.

What . . . Who did John see?
- Jesus.

What did John believe?
- Jesus is the Chosen One of God.

How can we be a witness for Jesus? How can we show we believe?
- children give examples.

What came from heaven and rested on Jesus?
- the Holy Spirit in the form of a dove.

SHARING

What do the pictures mean to the children?
- sharing life
- sharing jobs
- sharing games, etc.

In what ways did we share last week?
- have the children give examples.

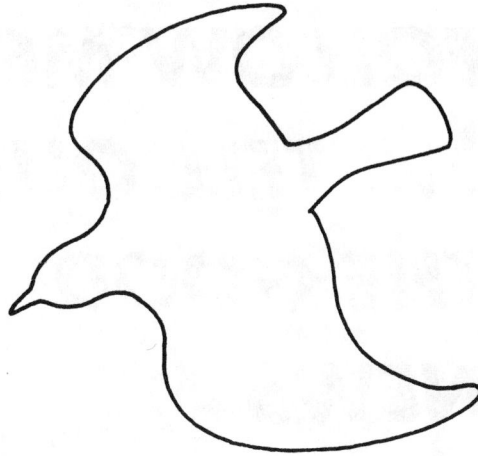

A reading from the Good News given to us by John.
Glory to you, Lord.

Jesus was walking by the River (Jordan).
His cousin (John) saw him, and said,
'Here is Jesus,
the (Lamb of God),
the Chosen One of God.'
Jesus asked John to (baptise) him in the River Jordan.

After baptising Jesus, John told everyone,
'I saw the Spirit come down from heaven like a (dove)
and rest on Jesus.
Yes, I have seen and I believe
that Jesus is the Chosen One of God.'

This is the Gospel of the Lord.
Praise to you, Lord Jesus Christ.

ACTIVITIES

> Give out the cut-out shapes.

> On them, have the children write or draw a prayer asking for the help of the Holy Spirit throughout the coming week, as they try to be witnesses to Jesus by their love.

> Have the children take it in turns to mime a person who is a witness to Jesus today, e.g. Mother Teresa.

FOLLOW ME . . . TELL OUT THE GOOD NEWS

VISUAL AIDS

> Seashells, fishing nets.

> Pictures of the seashore, fishing boats, fishermen;
and pictures of sick people, blind, lame, etc.

> Shell shape cut-outs.

WELCOME AND PROCLAIM THE GOSPEL

Say/sing together:

**Alleluia, alleluia!
Jesus told out the Good News
of the Kingdom,
and cured many people.
Alleluia!**

Today some of the words of the Gospel will be left out deliberately; listen carefully and fill them in.

The words to be omitted during the proclamation are presented in brackets.

DISCUSSION

Does anyone know the answer to the riddle?
- Jesus went walking on the seashore;
- he called fishermen to follow him;
- he told out the Good News;
- he cured the sick.

What did Jesus ask everyone to do?
- to turn to God.

What is the Good News?
- sight for the blind, etc.

Ask the children for examples of Good News in their lives; get them to say what it meant to them
- e.g. a new baby;
- e.g. Gran coming to visit, etc.

SHARING

Today we have a riddle:
what is the connection between
seashells, fishing nets, fishermen;
and sick people?

Listen carefully to the Gospel,
because it will give us the answer
to the riddle.

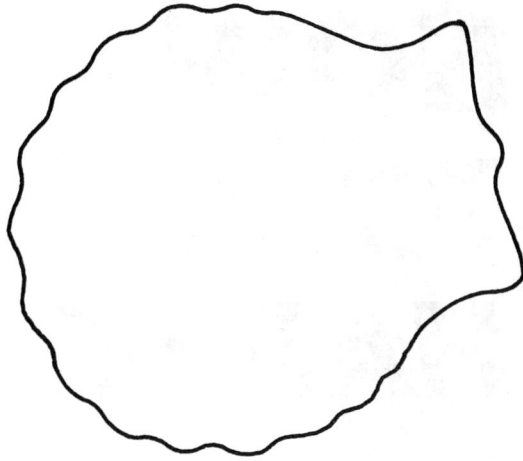

A reading from the Good News
given to us by Matthew.
Glory to you, Lord.

Jesus went to live in Capernaum, a
little seaside town. There Jesus told
out the message:
'The Kingdom of God is near,
turn to God.'
As Jesus walked by the seashore he
saw two brothers, fishermen, (Peter)
and (Andrew), casting their nets into
the lake. Jesus said to them,
'Follow me. I will make you
fishers of men.'
At once they left their nets and
followed him.
Jesus went round all Galilee,
teaching the people, telling out
the Good News, and curing all
kinds of sick people.

This is the Gospel of the Lord.
Praise to you, Lord Jesus Christ.

ACTIVITIES
> Have the children mime the
  Gospel:
  - Jesus on the shore, calling the
  fishermen, who then follow . . .
  - Jesus teaching the people,
  curing the sick, telling out the
  Good News . . .
> Give out the shell shapes.
> Have the children write or draw
  on them either:
  how they will tell out the Good
News by the way they follow
Jesus in the week ahead;
or what they would be happy to
leave behind to follow Jesus.
Fasten the drawings onto the
fishing net.
> When does Jesus call us to leave
  something for him?
  - leave a game to have dinner;
  - leave TV to do homework.
  Have the children give examples.

HOW TO BE HAPPY

VISUAL AIDS

> Pictures of people happily engaged in various activities.

> Several card sets of the individual words of the theme:
'HOW'; 'TO'; 'BE'; 'HAPPY'.

WELCOME AND PROCLAIM THE GOSPEL

Say/sing together:

Alleluia, alleluia!
Father, let your face shine on us.
Keep us in your love.
Alleluia!

A reading from the Good News given to us by Matthew.
Glory to you, Lord.

Crowds of people were following Jesus, trying to see him and hear him speak.
When Jesus saw the crowds, he climbed a little hill, where he sat down.
His friends joined him, and he began to tell the people how to be happy:

DISCUSSION

What ways of being happy did Jesus give?

Do the children know of any people who are happy in these ways?

How can we be happy in any one of the ways?

SHARING

Give out the sets of cards which the children have to rearrange to find the message.

Ask the children to talk about the happiest time or event they can remember. Why did it make them happy?

Sing a joyful song to thank God for happy times.

Today Jesus tells how we can be happy always.

'Happiness is being gentle.
Happiness is wanting God in your life.
Happiness is longing for what is right.
Happiness is being generous always.
Happiness is putting God first.
Happiness is being a peace-maker.
Happiness is standing up for God.
Happiness is suffering for God.

Rejoice and be glad, your reward will be very great in heaven.'

This is the Gospel of the Lord.
Praise to you, Lord Jesus Christ.

ACTIVITIES

> Divide the children into groups, and have them mime the ways of happiness.

> Prepare happiness posters or badges:
  - 'Happiness is . . .'
  - 'Happiness is being . . .'

SHINE LIKE A LIGHT

VISUAL AIDS

> Things mentioned in the Gospel: salt; various lights, e.g. torch; table-lamp; lampstand and bucket.
> Baptismal candle.
> Several card sets of the individual words: 'LET'; 'YOUR'; 'GOODNESS'; 'SHINE'; 'LIKE'; 'A'; 'LIGHT'.
> Candle shape cut-outs.

WELCOME AND PROCLAIM THE GOSPEL

Say/sing together:

Alleluia, alleluia!
Jesus is the Light of the world.
All who follow him
have the light of life.
Alleluia!

Use the visual aids as appropriate during the proclamation of the Gospel.

DISCUSSION

At Baptism we were each given a lighted candle, a sign of the light of Jesus. We were asked to keep the light of Jesus burning brightly. We keep our light burning brightly by the love we have for one another. When we love everyone we show that we are friends of Jesus.

ACTIVITIES

> Give each child a cut-out candle to colour. Encourage them to make the flames very bright!

> Have the children write or draw how they will let their light shine in the coming week.

> Introduce and use the psalm:

SHARING

Give out the card sets which the children have to rearrange to find the message.

Today Jesus tells us that there are two things we cannot do without. From the visual aids, have the children guess what they are.

On a large piece of paper make two columns: one for salt; the other for light. As the children offer reasons why they are so important, put a tick in the appropriate column.

A reading from the Good News given to us by Matthew.
Glory to you, Lord.

Jesus says to his friends:
'You are the salt of the earth.
But if salt loses its taste, what can make it salty again?
It is no good for anything except to be thrown out and trampled upon.

You are the light of the world.

When you light a lamp, you put it high on a lampstand, where it will give light for all the people of the house.
You do not hide it under a bucket.
Let your light shine,
then everyone will know what God means to you,
and they will give him praise.'

This is the Gospel of the Lord.
Praise to you, Lord Jesus Christ.

All say the response between verses, standing up straight and stretching their hands above their heads. Groups take it in turn to say the verses.
Response: **Being good is like being a light in the darkness.**
Those who are good are like lights in the darkness;
they are generous, merciful and just.
They look after the poor and the needy.
They live their lives with care. *Resp.*

Those who are just will never waver.
They will be remembered forever.
They have no fear of bad news.
They trust the Lord in their hearts.
Resp.
Their love is steady, no need to fear.
They give open-handedly to the poor.
You can count on them to be just always.
Their heads will be raised high in glory. *Resp.*

LOVE IS HIS WAY

VISUAL AIDS

> A variety of signs:
  - 'Close the door'; 'Quiet please'; 'Exit'; 'Mind the step'; etc.

> Picture of happy group of people.

> Star shape cut-outs.

> Tape of peaceful music.

WELCOME AND PROCLAIM THE GOSPEL

Say/sing together:

**Alleluia, alleluia!
Speak, Lord, we are listening.
Your Word will bring us life.
Alleluia!**

A reading from the Good News given to us by Matthew.
Glory to you, Lord.

Jesus says to his friends:
'I love you all very much.
I want you to be happy.

Let everything you do be guided by God's law of love.

Do good to everyone you meet.

DISCUSSION

What a wonderful world we would have if everyone lived God's law of love!

- by doing good to everyone;
- by respecting everyone;
- by keeping our promises.

Jesus' words are like stars guiding us towards heaven.

It is hard to do things we don't like. How can we make hard things easier?
- by practice, e.g. for swimming, music, sports, sums, etc.

How does Jesus want us to be happy?

SHARING

Children look at the signs, and suggest others.

Why do we have signs - little laws?
- to help and protect us.
How do they protect us?

Jesus tells us about signs or little laws which help us to love each other.

Respect everyone.
Keep your promises.'

This is the Gospel of the Lord.
Praise to you, Lord Jesus Christ.

ACTIVITIES

> Play peaceful music.

> Invite children to sit comfortably and think of something they find hard to do.

> Then to think of Jesus on the cross, and to tell him that they will try to do it for him.

> Give each child a cut-out star on which to write or draw a prayer for help with whatever it is they find hard.

LISTEN!

VISUAL AIDS

> Objects, or pictures of objects that produce sound, or that transmit sound:
  - e.g. musical instruments, radio, etc.

> Pictures of people listening.

> Heart shape cut-outs.

WELCOME AND PROCLAIM THE WORD

Say/sing together:

Alleluia, alleluia!
Lord, give us listening hearts.
Alleluia!

A reading from the Good News given to us by Matthew.
Glory to you, Lord.

'Listen!', said Jesus, 'Listen really hard!
Love your enemies.
Be good; be kind; be loving.
If someone hits you, do not hit back.
Share your things with everyone,
even with people you do not like;
even with those who steal, or break,

DISCUSSION

What does Jesus say to those who listen?
- love your enemies, etc.

How do we know when people have listened?
- by the kind of people they are;
- by the way they love and care for others they show they are listening with their hearts.

ACTIVITIES

> Have the children act out little scenes showing people behaving as if they have listened to Jesus with their hearts:
  - sharing things, e.g. sweets;
  - inviting people to play, forgiving, etc.

> Give out the heart shape cut-outs.

SHARING

Show the children the objects and the pictures.

Ask what their favourite sounds are: what do they like to listen to?

Ask them to be as quiet as possible and listen for the sounds around them: how many can they hear?

Play a 'listening' game: while all the others close their eyes, one child makes a noise, and they have to identify it. The winner who guesses the sound correctly takes the next turn to make another sound.

For the great gift of hearing and the world's wonderful sounds sing thanks and praise to God with a nice 'noisy' Gloria, e.g. with lots of percussion!

or spoil your things.

Treat everyone with love and kindness, just as you would like them to treat you.

Love everyone, not just those who are loving and kind to you.'

This is the Gospel of the Lord.
Praise to you, Lord Jesus Christ.

> On them have the children write or draw:
> either, ways in which they will listen next week;
> or, someone to whom they will listen better.

> Say the prayer, the children repeating it phrase by phrase:

**Thank you, heavenly Father,
for the song of the birds;
for the sound of the sea;
for the homely sounds of baby
  crying;
and mummy calling me in for tea;
for daddy's laugh and the sound of
  his feet
when he comes home at night.
Thank you, Father, for the sounds
  in the night,
when I'm all tucked up tight.**

WE ARE PRECIOUS TO GOD

VISUAL AIDS

> Pictures of flowers, birds, people in regalia.

> Cut-outs in the shape of flowers, birds, hearts.

WELCOME AND PROCLAIM THE GOSPEL

Say/sing together:

Alleluia, alleluia!
Your word is truth, O Lord.
Keep us true to you.
Alleluia!

A reading from the Good News given to us by Matthew.
Glory to you, Lord.

Jesus says:
'Do not worry about anything.
Do not worry about everyday things,
like what you are going to have for dinner, or what clothes you are going to wear.
These things are not important.
Life is much more important than

DISCUSSION

What does Jesus say about us?
- we are precious in God's eyes.
What does he ask us to do?
- set our hearts on God's Kingdom.
How do we do this?
- by loving God, and other people;
- by not worrying about money, about food, about clothes.

ACTIVITIES

> Give out the cut-out shapes.

> On them have the children write or draw and colour how they will set their hearts on God's Kingdom in the coming week.

> Recite the psalm, different groups saying a verse, all saying the response.

SHARING

Jesus tells us how much God loves and cares for us. He will never let anything harm us.

In this very old prayer-poem, we hear how being loved by God is like being safe inside a strong fortress.

Teach the response and pray the psalm (below) together:

food and clothes.
Look at the birds in the sky:
do they worry?
Do they plant and harvest?
Yet your heavenly Father feeds them.
Look all around you at the flowers:
look at their beautiful colours and shapes.
Do they worry?
Do they spend their days making clothes?

Yet not even Solomon, the richest of Kings, was dressed as
splendidly as a simple flower.
If God cares so much for these,
he cares much, much more for you
who are so precious to him.
So do not worry;
set your heart on God's Kingdom,
and God will take care of you.'

This is the Gospel of the Lord.
Praise to you, Lord Jesus Christ.

Response:
In God alone I am safe.

In God alone is my soul at rest;
my help comes from him.
He is my rock, my stronghold,
my fortress. I stand firm. *Response*

In God alone is my soul at rest;
my hope comes from him.
He is my rock, my stronghold,
my fortress. I stand firm. *Response*

In God alone is my safety and glory;
he is my rock of strength.
He is my shelter.
I trust him at all times. *Response*

BUILD ON LOVE

VISUAL AIDS

> Tray of sand, and a largish rock.

> A couple of jugs of water.

> Building blocks.

> House shape cut-outs.

WELCOME AND PROCLAIM THE WORD

Say/sing together:

Alleluia, alleluia!
If you love me, keep my word.
Then my Father will come
and make his home with you.
Alleluia!

A reading from the Good News given to us by Matthew.
Glory to you, Lord.

Jesus says:
'It is no good going around saying you love God if you do not do anything about it.
If you love God, you must show this love in your lives.
Listen to me and try to do as I say, and you will be like the wise man

DISCUSSION

What happened in the story?
- invite comments from the children.

How can we stand firm in God's love?
- by listening to Jesus
- by doing what Jesus says.

SHARING

Children take turns to:

- build on the sand with the blocks; pour the water on the sand and watch the blocks fall down as the sand is washed away;

- build on the rock; pour the water on the rock and watch what happens.

(Be careful that the water pours on the sand/rock, not onto the blocks.)

Make up a caption to describe the experiment.

Jesus says that just as the house is safe when it is built on rock, so we are safe on the rock of God's love.

who built his house on rock.
When the rains came
and the gales roared
and the floods rose
his house did not fall down.
It stood there safe and sound
because it was built on rock.

If you do not listen to me
you will be like the foolish man
who built his house on sand.
When the rains came

and the gales roared
and the floods rose
his house fell down
because it was built on sand.'

This is the Gospel of the Lord.
Praise to you, Lord Jesus Christ.

ACTIVITIES

> Give out the house shape cut-outs.

> Have the children colour them and write or draw how they will build on the rock of God's love in the week ahead.

FOLLOW JESUS

VISUAL AIDS

> Pictures of roads, trains, ships, cars, luggage, people travelling.

> Heart shape cut-outs.

WELCOME AND PROCLAIM THE GOSPEL

Say/sing together:

Alleluia, alleluia!
Father, open our hearts
to hear the call of Jesus.
Alleluia!

A reading from the Good News given to us by Matthew.
Glory to you, Lord.

As Jesus was walking he passed the custom house where the people went to pay their taxes. A man was sitting there, collecting the taxes. His name was Matthew.

'Matthew', Jesus called, 'follow me.' At once Matthew jumped up,

DISCUSSION

How did Matthew celebrate being called by Jesus?
- he gave a party.

Who did he invite?
- Jesus
- his tax collector friends, who collected money for the Romans.

What did the Jewish leaders say?
- 'Why is Jesus mixing with bad people?'

How did Jesus reply?
- 'I have come to call sinners.'

Who are Jesus' followers today?
- we are.

SHARING

Encourage the children to talk about:

- journeys they have made;
- reasons for travelling;
- modes of transport;
- feelings.

left all the money on the table and ran after Jesus.

Matthew invited Jesus to a meal at his house.
Lots of Matthew's friends, who were also tax collectors, came along.
Some Jewish leaders saw this, and asked the followers of Jesus why their master ate with such bad people.

Jesus heard them and said,
'I have not come
to call those who are good,
but to call sinners.'

This is the Gospel of the Lord.
Praise to you, Lord Jesus Christ.

ACTIVITIES

Do we have to wait until we are good, or grown up, or famous to follow Jesus?
- we can follow Jesus now
- we can be like Matthew, who followed Jesus in love
- we do the best we can out of love.

> Have the children mime the Gospel.

> Give out the heart shape cut-outs.

> On them have the children write or draw how they will follow Jesus in love in the week ahead.

SERVE THE LORD WITH GLADNESS

VISUAL AIDS

> Picture of the apostles, especially at the Last Supper.

> People shape cut-outs.

WELCOME AND PROCLAIM THE GOSPEL

Say/sing together:

Alleluia, alleluia!
My friends listen to my voice,
says Jesus.
I know them and they know me.
Alleluia!

A reading from the Good News given to us by Matthew.
Glory to you, Lord.

Jesus felt sorry for the great crowd of people that had come to listen to him because there was no one to help them.
'They are just like scattered sheep', said Jesus, 'who have no shepherd to guide them.'

DISCUSSION

What did Jesus give to his friends?
- the power to conquer evil;
- the power to cure sickness.

Ask what the children know about each apostle.

We too are called to be Jesus' friends.

What power does he give us?
- the power to love;
- the power to forgive;
- the power to share.

SHARING

Today we have a picture of some of Jesus' special friends:
- the twelve apostles;
- have the children name them.

Last week we heard how Jesus called Matthew. Listen today as he calls more special friends to follow him.

So Jesus called his friends together, and gave them the power they needed to help the people:
the power to conquer evil;
the power to cure all kinds of sickness.

These are the names of Jesus' twelve friends:
Peter; Andrew; James; John; Philip; Bartholomew; Thomas; Matthew; James; Thaddeus; Simon and Judas.

This is the Gospel of the Lord.
Praise to you, Lord Jesus Christ.

ACTIVITIES

> Give out the people shape cut-outs.

> Have the children colour the person to represent themselves.

> Have the children write or draw on the front of the 'person' how they will be Jesus' friend in the week ahead.

DO NOT BE AFRAID

VISUAL AIDS

> Hair.

> Pictures of sparrows.

> Sparrow shape cut-outs.

WELCOME AND PROCLAIM THE GOSPEL

Say/sing together:

**Alleluia, alleluia!
Jesus gives us the power
to be his friends.
Alleluia!**

A reading from the Good News given to us by Matthew.
Glory to you, Lord.

Jesus says:
'You need never be afraid of anything.
Things will go wrong,
and it will be hard for my friends,
but there is no need to be afraid,
not even of people who can kill you.

DISCUSSION

What does Jesus say about fears?
- do not be afraid.

What are we afraid of?
- spiders, the dark . . .

What does Jesus say to us about these fears we have?
- 'God knows about it; he will look after you.'

How well does God know us?
- he knows how many hairs we each have on our head.

Can you count how many hairs you have?

How valuable are we to God?
- worth more than hundreds of sparrows, and if God looks after sparrows, how much more he cares for us.

SHARING

Have the children recall and talk about wonderful things that have happened to them and their families.

And yet we grumble more than we manage to say 'thank you'.

Make up a litany, with each child adding an intention:
'Thank you, God, for . . .'.

In today's Gospel Jesus is telling his friends how much God loves them.

We too are Jesus' friends, and he is speaking to us as well.

You can buy sixteen sparrows for a penny, but if one falls to the ground and dies, God, your loving Father, knows all about it.

Every hair on your head has been counted. There is no need to be afraid. You are worth more than hundreds of sparrows.'

This is the Gospel of the Lord.
Praise to you, Lord Jesus Christ.

ACTIVITIES

> Give out the sparrow shape cut-outs.

> On them have the children write or draw:
  something of which they are afraid;
  and a prayer asking for God's help.

WELCOME, JESUS!

VISUAL AIDS

> A cup of cold water.

> Cup shape cut-outs.

WELCOME AND PROCLAIM THE WORD

Say/sing together:

Alleluia, alleluia!
Open our hearts, Lord,
to welcome your friends.
Alleluia!

A reading from the Good News given to us by Matthew.
Glory to you, Lord.

Jesus says:
'My friends, choose me over and above anyone or anything else in this world.
Be willing to follow in my footsteps, even to carrying a cross like me.

DISCUSSION

What does Jesus expect of his friends?
- to choose him over and above everything else
- to follow in his footsteps
- to carry a cross.

How does Jesus expect his friends to be treated?
- to be made welcome.

When we welcome a friend of Jesus, we welcome Jesus.

If we welcome everyone we will be sure of welcoming Jesus and his friends.

SHARING

Who are the people who make us feel welcome?
- children who want to share their games and toys;
- children at school who let us join in their games.

How well do we make others feel welcome?

- little brothers or sisters who want to join in our games;
- visitors who come to our house.

God makes everyone welcome; he never turns away anyone who comes to him.

Today Jesus tells his friends more about what it means to be his friend.

Anyone who makes my friends welcome is welcoming me.

Even if it is only a cup of cold water that you give to my friends, you will be rewarded.'

This is the Gospel of the Lord.
Praise to you, Lord Jesus Christ.

ACTIVITIES

> Give out the cup shape cut-outs.

> Have the children write or draw on them how they will fill the cups with loving welcomes in the week ahead.

COME TO ME

VISUAL AIDS

> Pictures of people carrying loads, pictures of yoked animals.

> Solemn sounding music.

> Cheerful sounding music.

> Yoke shape cut-outs.

WELCOME AND PROCLAIM THE GOSPEL

Say/sing together:

**Alleluia, alleluia!
Bless you, Father,
for showing the truth to children.
Alleluia!**

A reading from the Good News given to us by Matthew.
Glory to you, Lord.

Jesus says:

'I praise and bless you, Father,
Lord of heaven and earth,
for hiding your secrets from the wise and learned,
and sharing them with children.
You have trusted me with everything.

DISCUSSION

With whom does God share his secrets?
- with children.

To whom does Jesus make God known?
- those whom Jesus chooses.

What does Jesus offer in exchange for a heavy burden?

- rest and comfort.

What advice does Jesus give and why?
- to carry his burden instead
- because it is easy and light.

What is Jesus' burden and his yoke?
- love
- his yoke binds us to him and each other.

SHARING

Look at the pictures. Get the children to say what they do like carrying, and what they do not like carrying.

What does 'burden' mean?
- something too hard, too heavy.

What does 'yoke' mean?
- to link together,
- could be as slave, or as in love.

Play the solemn music and have the children mime pulling a heavy load. Play the cheerful music and have the children mime pulling a light load.

It is easy for strong people to carry heavy loads. Strong people train. We can be trained, but training is hard work. It is much easier to remain weak and let someone else carry the load for us, for example leaving others to wash up, make the beds.

I know my Father, and I will help those whom I choose to know him.

If your burden is heavy, come to me, and I will give you rest and comfort. Put my yoke on your shoulders. My yoke is easy and my burden is light.'

This is the Gospel of the Lord.
Praise to you, Lord Jesus Christ.

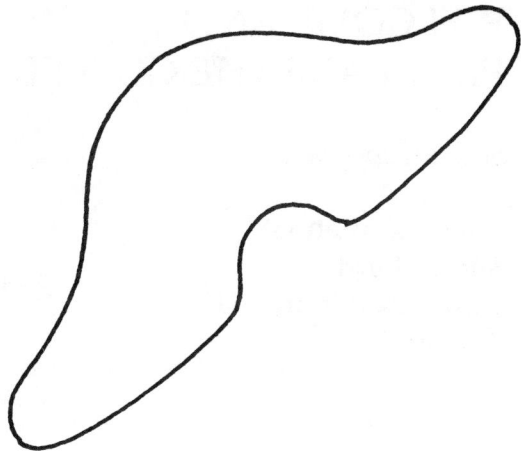

ACTIVITIES

> Give out the yoke shape cut-outs.

> Ask the children to write or draw on them how they can give someone rest and comfort in the week ahead.

> Recite the following prayer, the children repeating it line by line:

**Lord, you are faithful
in all that you say,
and loving in all that you do.**

**Support all who fall,
comfort the burdened,
and help all
who come to you for help.**

LISTEN!

VISUAL AIDS

> Seeds, wheat, weeds, thorns, withered plants, rocks.

> Seed shape cut-outs.

WELCOME AND PROCLAIM THE GOSPEL

Say/sing together:

**Alleluia, alleluia!
Speak, Lord,
your servants are listening.
Alleluia!**

A reading from the Good News given to us by Matthew.
Glory to you, Lord.

Jesus says:
'Imagine that you are a farmer going out to sow your seeds.
As you sow, some seeds fall on the pathway, where the birds swoop down and eat them up.
Some seeds fall among the rocks where there is hardly any soil;

DISCUSSION

When are we like the seeds:
- that fall on the path?
- that fall amongst rocks?
- that fall amongst thorns and weeds?
- that fall on good soil?

ACTIVITIES

> Have the children mime the story, taking turns to be the farmer, the seed, the birds, the weeds, etc.

> Give out the seed shape cut-outs.

> Have the children write or draw the good crop that they will produce in the week ahead.

SHARING

Invite the children to close their eyes, and listen to the sounds all around them.

What sounds did they hear last week?

Which of those sounds did they like, and which ones did they not like?

Today Jesus is sitting by the lakeside, talking to a great crowd of people; listen to him.

they soon wither away because they can not put down good roots.
Some seeds fall among the thorns and weeds, and get smothered and choked by them.
Some seeds fall on good ground with rich soil, where they will grow up strong and produce a good crop.'

This is the Gospel of the Lord.
Praise to you, Lord Jesus Christ.

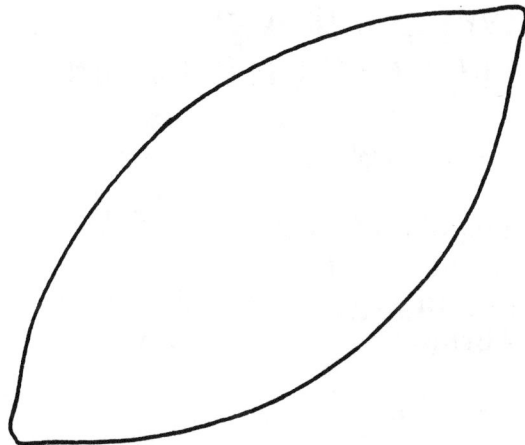

> Recite the psalm, all saying the response, individuals or groups the verses:

Response:
Help us, Lord, to grow in rich soil.

Lord, you take great care of the
  earth.
You fill it with wonderful things.
Your river in heaven overflows
to provide us with grain. *Response*

You provide for the earth,
you water it with rain.
You soften the earth with gentle rain.
You bless its growth. *Response*

The hills rejoice,
the meadows are full of sheep.
Wheat fills the valleys.
The whole world shouts for joy.
                    Response

THE KINGDOM OF HEAVEN IS LIKE . . .

VISUAL AIDS

> Cultivated plants, weeds, picture of a barn.

> Outline picture of a barn.

> Seed shape cut-outs.

WELCOME AND PROCLAIM THE GOSPEL

Say/sing together:

**Alleluia, alleluia!
Help us, Lord,
to grow in goodness and love.
Alleluia!**

A reading from the Good News given to us by Matthew.
Glory to you, Lord.

Jesus says:
'Imagine that you are a farmer. You go out and sow a whole field with good seed. But then in the night, while you are asleep, an enemy comes, sows lots of weeds in your field, and runs away. The good seed begins to grow

DISCUSSION

Next week we can sow good or bad seed: - how?

We can be good seed or we can be bad seed: - how?

What is the field? - the world.

What is the barn? - heaven.

SHARING

Reflect with the children how good and bad go on together all the time: people loving, people fighting.

Encourage the children to think of examples.

Today Jesus tells another story about the farmer. Listen to what happens to him this week.

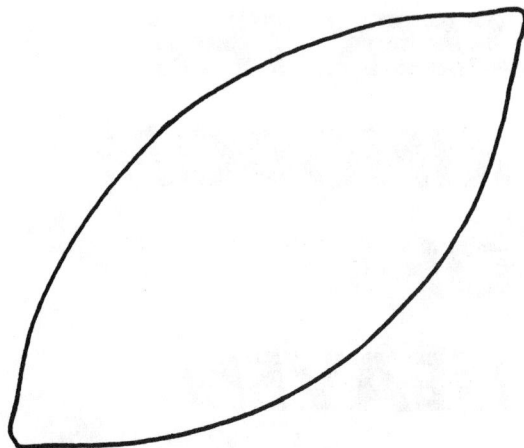

beautifully, but mixed up with the good plants are crowds of weeds, spiky, chokey, prickly weeds. "Where did all these weeds come from?" asked the farmer. "I sowed good seed. An enemy must have done this to cause me trouble." The farmer's men wanted to go and pull up all the weeds, but the farmer stopped them. "Leave them to grow together in case you damage the good plants by pulling out the weeds. Wait until harvest time, and we'll cut them all down. But we'll put the good crop in the barn, and burn the weeds.'"

This is the Gospel of the Lord.
Praise to you, Lord Jesus Christ.

ACTIVITIES

> Have the children mime the Gospel.

> Give out the cut-out shapes.

> On them have the children write or draw how they will sow good seed in the week ahead.

> Give out blank paper and have the children draw how they will grow into good plants. Gather the work into the 'barn'.

SEEK THE KINGDOM OF HEAVEN

VISUAL AIDS

> Treasure box, pearls, fishing net; or pictures of these.

> Cut-out shapes of pearls, fishes.

> A basket.

WELCOME AND PROCLAIM THE GOSPEL

Say/sing together:

**Alleluia, alleluia!
I call you friends
because I have shared
all my Father's secrets with you.
Alleluia!**

A reading from the Good News given to us by Matthew.
Glory to you, Lord.

Jesus says:
'The Kingdom of heaven is like a treasure hidden in a field. One day a man found the treasure, but hid it again so that no one else could find it. He went off and sold everything he had to buy the field.
The Kingdom of heaven is like a

DISCUSSION

What happened in each of the three stories?

What links the three stories?
- keep what is worth having, and let all the rest go.

What gift has God given us to help us find his treasure?
- the gift of faith.

What is it that faith helps us find?
- to find the Kingdom of God everywhere in the world around us;
- helps us to see what is really valuable and what is really rubbish.

The Kingdom is?
- love, kindness, truth . . .
The rubbish is?
- hate, stealing, nastiness . . .

SHARING

Ask what the children value most in life:
- what are their dreams?
- what are they willing to do to make their dreams come true?

Explore together examples of other people's hopes, aims, dreams, and how they have made them come true.

For example:
- to win an Olympic medal
- to climb a mountain
- to run a marathon.

Everything else has to be sacrificed.

Today Jesus tells us three stories about choosing and picking what is really valuable.

merchant searching for rare pearls. One day he discovered a pearl of great value, the largest, most beautiful he had ever seen. Nothing would make him happy until it was his, so he too sold everything he had until he had enough money to buy the pearl. The Kingdom of Heaven is like a fishing net thrown into the sea by the fishermen. When they pull it back into the boat it is full of fish:

big fish, small fish, fat fish, thin fish, good fish, bad fish. The fishermen sit down on the shore and sort the fish out; the good fish they collect into baskets; the rest they throw away.'

This is the Gospel of the Lord.
Praise to you, Lord Jesus Christ.

ACTIVITIES

> Let the children choose from the different cut-out shapes.

> Have the children draw or write on the shape how they can seek the Kingdom in the week ahead.

> Have the children gather pearls into the box; fish into the basket.

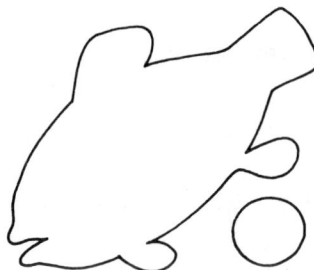

> Divide the children into groups to mime the stories.

HOW GOOD GOD IS

VISUAL AIDS

> Bread and sardines.

> Pictures of large crowds, rich and poor people.

> Bread shape and fish shape cut-outs.

WELCOME AND PROCLAIM THE GOSPEL

Say/sing together:

**Alleluia, alleluia!
Anyone who comes to me
will never be hungry.
Alleluia!**

A reading from the Good News given to us by Matthew.
Praise to you, Lord Jesus Christ.

After John the Baptist was put to death Jesus and his friends wanted to be quiet and alone. They went by boat to a lonely place.
But when they stepped ashore, a huge crowd was already there. Jesus took pity on them, and healed the sick.

DISCUSSION

How much food did Jesus and his friends have?

What did Jesus do with it?

What does Jesus want us to do?
- share
- trust him.

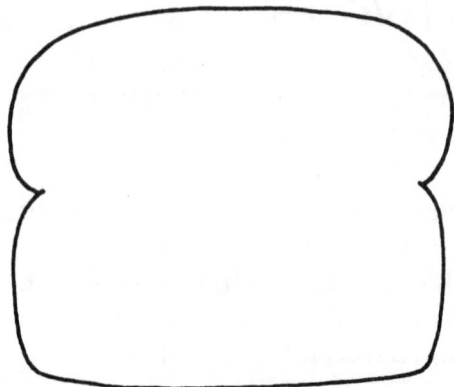

18th SUNDAY IN ORDINARY TIME

SHARING

If everyone shared what little they had, there would be plenty for everyone.

Ask the children what they have that they can share.

When do they find it difficult to share?

Look at the pictures, and get the children to comment on the differences between rich and poor.

Today's Gospel story is about sharing.

Time slipped by and soon it was evening. The people were hungry. 'What shall we do?' asked Jesus' friends. 'There are no shops. Shall we send these people to villages to buy food?'
'No', said Jesus, 'you can feed the people yourselves.'
'But we only have five loaves and two fishes! That's not enough to share!'
'Give it to me', said Jesus, 'and ask the people to sit down.'
Jesus took the bread and fish, blessed them, broke the bread, and gave it to his friends. They shared it with the people, and everyone had plenty to eat. When they gathered up the scraps afterwards, they filled twelve baskets.

This is the Gospel of the Lord.
Praise to you, Lord Jesus Christ.

ACTIVITIES

> Read the Gospel again, and have the children mime to it.

> Give out the loaf and fish shapes.

> Have the children write or draw on the cut-outs what they have that they can share:
  - hands to help
  - feet to run messages . . .

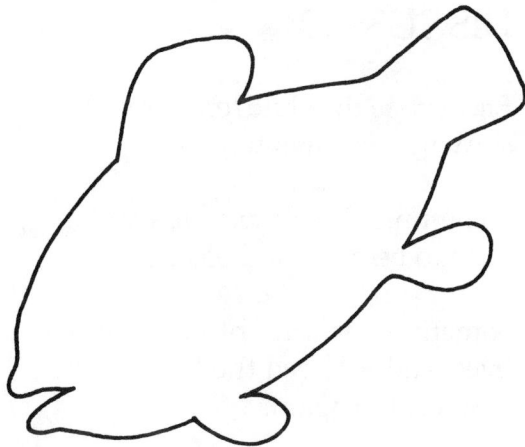

TRULY, YOU ARE THE SON OF GOD

VISUAL AIDS

> Pictures of calm sea and stormy sea, and of boats.

> Boat shape cut-outs.

> Quiet music.

WELCOME AND PROCLAIM THE GOSPEL

Say/sing together:

Alleluia, alleluia!
Truly, you are the Son of God.
Alleluia!

A reading from the Good News given to us by Matthew.
Glory to you, Lord.

Jesus had gone up into the hills to pray, and his friends set out to cross the lake by boat. Suddenly, when they were far out, a storm blew up. The little boat was tossed up and down in the giant waves. It was dark and Jesus' friends were very afraid.

DISCUSSION

Encourage the children to retell the story in their own words.

Sometimes, like Jesus, we want or need to be quiet and alone.

Sometimes 'storms' blow up in our lives, and we need the help of Jesus to find calm again.

Have the children give examples of times when Jesus comes to help us, but we do not always recognise him; or we fail to believe in him because he does not come in a way we expect.

SHARING

Encourage the children to share their experiences of the sea, or films/ books about the sea.

Today's Gospel story is about a storm on a huge lake.

Then they saw someone walking towards them across the stormy sea. They were terrified, thinking it was a ghost.
'It is I. Do not be afraid', a voice called out. Peter shouted
'Is that you, Lord? If it is, let me come to you across the water.'
'Come!', said the voice. Peter climbed out of the tossing boat on to the stormy waves and started walking across the water. But when he felt the wind tearing at him, he became frightened and began to sink. He shouted out,
'Lord, save me!' Immediately Jesus stretched out and caught Peter.
'Why did you doubt me?', Jesus said. They climbed into the boat. The wind dropped and all was calm again. Amazed, they all said
'Truly, you are the Son of God.'
This is the Gospel of the Lord.
Praise to you, Lord Jesus Christ.

ACTIVITIES

> Play quiet music while the children sit calm and comfortably, and pray for the faith they need to recognise/believe in Jesus.

> Give out the boat shape cut-outs.

> Have the children write or draw on them how they want Jesus to help them.

LET ALL PEOPLES PRAISE YOU, GOD

VISUAL AIDS

> Three candles.

> At least three pictures of peoples of different nationalities, from different countries.

WELCOME AND PROCLAIM THE GOSPEL

Say/sing together:

Alleluia, alleluia!
Lord, increase our faith.
Alleluia!

A reading from the Good News given to us by Matthew.
Glory to you, Lord.

One day as Jesus was travelling through the countryside a foreign woman came out and shouted, 'Son of David, have mercy on me! My daughter is tormented by a devil!'
Jesus did not answer her, so the woman kept following him. The

DISCUSSION

What was the woman asking for?

Why did Jesus grant her request?

Do we have faith when we pray?

When do we need faith?

When do we find it hard to pray?

ACTIVITIES

> Give the children blank pieces of paper. Either ask them to write or draw times when they need faith; or have them write a prayer asking God to strengthen their faith.

> Divide the children into groups to recite the verses of this psalm, everyone saying the response.

SHARING

What are the nationalities of the children in the group?
Which countries have they visited?
What do they know about other countries and their peoples?

Today's Gospel is about a foreign woman who came to Jesus.

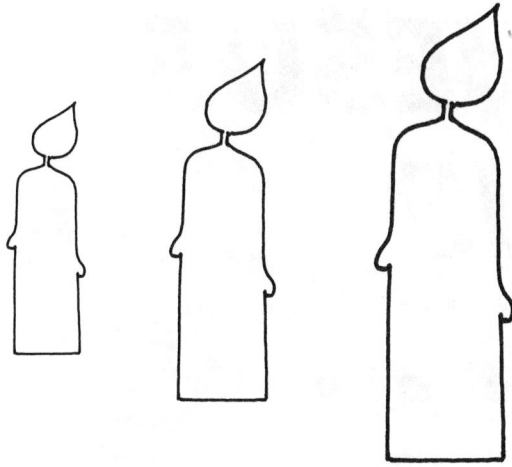

disciples were embarrassed by the woman, who kept shouting after them. They pleaded with Jesus to give her what she wanted, so she would go away.
'I was sent to help our own people', Jesus said.
The woman came up to Jesus, knelt at his feet and begged,
'Lord, help me!'
Jesus replied
'It's not fair to throw the children's food to the dogs.'
'But even the dogs can eat the scraps that fall from the master's table', she replied.
'Woman', said Jesus, 'you have great faith. Your prayer will be answered.'
And from that moment the woman's daughter was well again.

This is the Gospel of the Lord.
Praise to you, Lord Jesus Christ.

As each verse begins, light a candle in front of the picture of people of different nations.
Response:
Let all peoples praise you, God,
let all peoples praise you.

O God, be gracious and bless us,
may your face shed its light upon us.
May your ways be known on earth.
May all nations know your saving
help. *Response.*

Let the nations be glad and rejoice.
For you rule the world with justice.
You rule all peoples with fairness,
you guide the nations on earth.
Response.

Let the peoples praise you, O God,
let all the peoples praise you.
May God still give us his blessing
till the ends of the earth revere him.
Response.

JESUS IS

● ● ●

VISUAL AIDS

> Pictures of Saint Peter,
> of the Pope, and of Saint Peter's
> Basilica in Rome.

> A large key.

> Key shape cut-outs.

WELCOME AND PROCLAIM THE GOSPEL

Say/sing together:

**Alleluia, alleluia!
You are Christ,
Son of the living God.
Alleluia!**

A reading from the Good News given to us by Matthew.
Glory to you, Lord.

One day Jesus asked his friends, 'Who do people say that I am?' They said to him that many people thought he was a prophet; perhaps one of the great prophets, like Elijah or Jeremiah come back to life. 'But you', Jesus asked them, 'who do you say that I am?'

DISCUSSION

What was the first question Jesus asked his friends?
- 'who do people say I am?'
What answers did they give?
- John the Baptist, Elijah, Jeremiah.
What did Jesus ask Peter?
- 'who do you say I am?'
What three things does Jesus then say to Peter?

- it is faith that let him see who Jesus really is;
- Jesus calls him 'Peter', the rock on which the church will be built;
- Jesus gives Peter the keys of the kingdom.
Discuss the meaning of 'Peter' (= rock); and the significance of keys.
Who found the answer to the three SHARING questions?

SHARING

Encourage the children to share what they know about Saint Peter.

What is the connection between Saint Peter and the present Pope? Who is the present Pope?

In pictures of Saint Peter you can usually find keys; why is this?

Today Jesus gives us some of the answers to our questions. Listen carefully, and see how many of the answers you can find.

Simon Peter spoke up firmly:
'You are the Christ, the Son of the living God.'
Then Jesus said to him,
'You should be happy, Simon Peter, because it is the faith that God our Father has given you that tells you who I am.
You are Peter and on this rock I will build my church.
I will give you the keys of the kingdom.'

This is the Gospel of the Lord.
Praise to you, Lord Jesus Christ.

ACTIVITIES

> Give out the key shape cut-outs.

> On one side of the shape have the children write or draw who Jesus is for them.
  On the other side of the key, have them write or draw:
  either, how they can be rocks of faith for Jesus;

or, how they can be kingdom people in the week ahead.

IS ANYTHING WORTH MORE THAN LIFE?

VISUAL AIDS

> Crucifix.

> Cross shape cut-outs.

WELCOME AND PROCLAIM THE GOSPEL

Say/sing together:

**Alleluia, alleluia!
Take up your cross and follow me.
Alleluia!**

A reading from the Good News given to us by Matthew.
Glory to you, Lord.

Jesus began explaining to his friends that he must go to Jerusalem, and that once he got there he would suffer a great deal; that he would even be put to death, but that he would rise from the dead on the third day.

DISCUSSION

What or who did Jesus' friends value?

What did Jesus say would happen to him? What did Peter say?

What did Jesus reply? And what did his reply mean?

Invite the children to give examples of when they find it hard to follow Jesus.

Is there anything worth more than life?

SHARING

Encourage the children to give examples of what they count as valuable, precious.

What sometimes happens to what people value?
It gets stolen, damaged, destroyed.

What do the children think is most precious to them?

How would they feel if they lost it?

How would they feel if they knew beforehand that something like this was going to happen?

That is how Jesus' friends feel in today's story: they want to prevent something damaging something precious to them.

But Peter would not listen, and began to argue with Jesus. 'Heaven preserve you, Lord. This mustn't be allowed to happen to you.'

Jesus said,
'Anyone who wants to be one of my followers must take their cross and follow me. Is there anything worth more than your life?'

This is the Gospel of the Lord.
Praise to you, Lord Jesus Christ.

ACTIVITIES

> Give out the cross shape cut-outs.

> Have the children write or draw a prayer asking Jesus to be the most precious, the most valuable person in their lives.

> Say this prayer together, the children repeating it line by line after you:

Loving Father,
fill our hearts with your love
and with the desire to please you
in all that we do with our lives.
Help us to know you more each
  day,
to love you more dearly,
to follow you more closely.
Help us when times are difficult
and the way is hard.
Let us have no fear
as we follow in your footsteps.

I WILL BE WITH YOU

VISUAL AIDS

> Pictures of people in groups, sharing some activity, e.g. a meal or a picnic.

WELCOME AND PROCLAIM THE GOSPEL

Say/sing together:

**Alleluia, alleluia!
Let us love one another
as Jesus loves us.
Alleluia!**

A reading from the Good News given to us by Matthew.
Glory to you, Lord.

Jesus says to his friends:
'I have something very important to say to you.

If two of you on earth agree to ask anything at all, my Father in heaven will grant it to you.

DISCUSSION

Jesus said he had something very important to say to us today; what was it?
- that if two or three agree . . .
- that where two or three meet in his name . . .

When do we meet in Jesus' name?
- in Church, on Sunday.

Where else?
- whenever we share, help, play together, show love, pray . . .
When do we not meet in Jesus' name?
- whenever we fight, quarrel, argue . . .

Jesus says there is nothing worth quarrelling over.

SHARING

Encourage the children to give examples of times when families and friends meet together. Prompt them by asking why and where.
- meet for parties, meals, etc., in each other's homes.

On Sundays the family of God, the friends of Jesus meet: where?
- in Church to hear God's word and to gather round his table.

Why?
- to thank and praise God for all he has done for us.

One great prayer of praise we use on a Sunday is the Gloria: let us say it together now to thank God for all the joy and happiness our families and friends give us.

Wherever two or three meet in my name, I shall be there with them.'

This is the Gospel of the Lord.
Praise to you, Lord Jesus Christ.

ACTIVITIES

> Give the children blank pieces of paper and ask them to write or draw:
ways they will meet together in Jesus' name throughout the next week;
ways of not meeting together in Jesus' name that they will avoid.

> Or the children could compose a prayer asking for Jesus' help to avoid quarrelling, arguing, fighting.

FORGIVE FROM YOUR HEART

VISUAL AIDS

> On individual cards, the letters of
F O R G I V E N E S S.
(If you have a large group, make several sets.)

> Heart shape cut-outs.

WELCOME AND PROCLAIM THE GOSPEL

Say/sing together:
**Alleluia, alleluia!
Forgive us
as we forgive others.
Alleluia!**

A reading from the Good News given to us by Matthew.
Glory to you, Lord.

Peter asked Jesus,
'Suppose someone does me wrong, how often must I forgive them?'
Jesus answered with this story:
'There once was a rich king, who decided to call in all the money owed to him. One man owed thousands of pounds. He couldn't possibly pay back, so the king ordered that the man be sold as a slave, and his wife and children too, and everything he owned, until the debt was paid. The

DISCUSSION

What happened in the story? Have the children retell the story in their own words.

What did Peter want to know?

Do we ever behave like anyone in the story?

ACTIVITIES

> Have the children mime the Gospel story.

> Give out the heart shape cut-outs.

> The children write a prayer thanking God for forgiving them.

> The children write how they will

SHARING

Give out the letters and challenge the children to find the word.
When they have found the word, ask them what it means.

Encourage them to define it by giving examples of forgiving and being forgiven.

When, and why, is it hard to forgive?

man threw himself at the king's feet, "Give me time", he pleaded, "and I'll pay back every penny I owe."
The king had pity, cancelled the whole debt, and let the man go free.
On his way home the man met a friend who owed him about a pound. He grabbed the man by the throat, and demanded
"Pay me back the money you owe!"
"Give me time", his friend pleaded.
But the man wouldn't listen, and had his friend thrown into prison.
When the king heard this, he was very upset and sent for the man.
"You wicked man! When you asked for mercy, I cancelled your debt - but you had no pity." And the king had the man thrown into prison.
So', said Jesus, 'God will deal with anyone who does not forgive from the heart.'
This is the Gospel of the Lord.
Praise to you, Lord Jesus Christ.

be forgiving, who they will forgive, in the week ahead.

GOD IS LOVE

VISUAL AIDS

> Pictures of vines/vineyard.
> Bunch of grapes.
> Clock face.
> Coin shape cut-outs.
> Time cards, enough to give each child one: they should have different times marked on them: 8.00 am; 12 noon; 4.00 pm; 6.00 pm.

WELCOME AND PROCLAIM THE GOSPEL

Say/sing together:
Alleluia, alleluia!
Lord, you are just and loving,
and your goodness lasts for ever.
Alleluia!

A reading from the Good News given to us by Matthew.
Glory to you, Lord.

Jesus told this story:
'The kingdom of heaven is like a farmer who went out very early in the morning to employ people to work in his vineyard. He agreed to pay them one pound a day, and sent them off to work.
At mid-day the farmer returned to the market place, and found other people there, looking for work. He promised he would give them a fair wage, so they too went off to work in

DISCUSSION

What happened in the story?
What is God telling us in the story?
- that God loves us more than the work we do
- that we each are more important to God than all the work in the world
- all we have is a gift from God
- do we deserve anything?
God looks after us out of love.

Encourage the children to give examples of God's gifts to them.

All God asks is that we do well what we have time for,
and that we do it for him with love.

SHARING

Encourage the children to give examples of fairness and unfairness. Have they ever been unfairly treated? How did they feel? Have they ever treated anyone else unfairly?

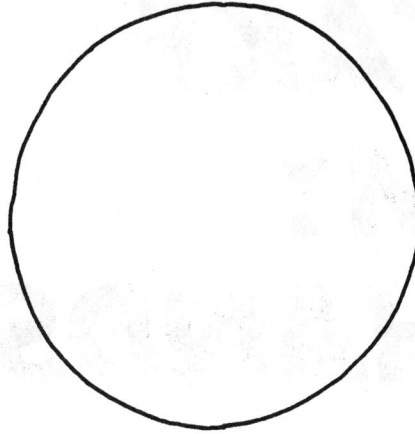

Sometimes the friends of Jesus felt that life was unfair to them. By way of reply, Jesus told them a story.

his vineyard.
At tea-time, the farmer went to the market-place again, found more people looking for work, so he sent these to work in his vineyard as well. And then, an hour before the day's work ended, the farmer went back to find still more people looking for work. These too went to work in his vineyard. At the end of the day, when the wages were to be given out, everyone was given a pound.

Those who had worked all day began to grumble.
"It's not fair! We worked all day, and got only as much as those who worked for just an hour!"
The farmer reminded them they had agreed to work for one pound when he hired them.
"Why grumble", he said, "because I choose to be generous?"'
This is the Gospel of the Lord.
Praise to you, Lord Jesus Christ.

ACTIVITIES

> Give each child a time card.

> Have the children mime the Gospel: the 'workers' will be hired according to the time on their cards.

> Give out the coin shape cut-outs.

> On them have the children write about or draw a gift for which they want to thank God.

TAKE MY HANDS

VISUAL AIDS

> Pictures of families, especially children playing, helping, sleeping.

WELCOME AND PROCLAIM THE GOSPEL

Say/sing together:

Alleluia, alleluia!
To love God is to hear his word
and to do his will.
Alleluia!

A reading from the Good News given to us by Matthew.
Glory to you, Lord.

Jesus told his friends this story:
'There once was a man who had two sons. One day the man said to one of his sons,
"My son, I want you to go and work in my vineyard today." The boy answered
"No, I won't!" And off he went. But

DISCUSSION

Who can answer Jesus' question?
The boy who said he wouldn't, but did?
Or the boy who said he would, but didn't?

Invite the children to retell the Gospel story, substituting present day examples of things that a parent might ask their children to do.

ACTIVITIES

> Have the children act out the Gospel story, if possible with a present day equivalent as revealed in the discussion.

> Give out blank pieces of paper, and ask the children to write or draw how they will respond in the coming week when asked to do something.

SHARING

Encourage the children to discuss what they see illustrated in the pictures.
Invite them to give examples of things that they do like doing, and things that they do not like doing; to give examples of jobs that they are asked to do, and to say how they react when asked.

Today Jesus tells the story of two boys who were asked by their father to do something they didn't really want to do. At the end of the story Jesus asks a question: listen carefully and be ready to answer it.

later in the day, he thought better of it, and went along to the vineyard to do the work his father had asked. Meantime the man called his second son and said
"My son, I want you to go and work in my vineyard today." The second son replied
"Certainly, Father." But he didn't go.'
Then Jesus said to his friends
'Which of these two sons did what his father wanted?'

This is the Gospel of the Lord.
Praise to you, Lord Jesus Christ.

> Or they might draw someone (parent, teacher, etc.) who might ask them to do something, and how they will respond.

> Say the following prayer together, the children repeating it line by line:

Lord Jesus,
your love for us is so great
that you did not refuse
to give up your whole life for us.
Help us to be generous,
so that we grow more like you each
    day.
Amen.

LORD, FILL US WITH YOUR LOVE

VISUAL AIDS

> Pictures of the splendours of creation.

> A bunch of grapes.

> Grape shape cut-outs.

WELCOME AND PROCLAIM THE GOSPEL

Say/sing together:

Alleluia, alleluia!
Lord, we belong to you.
Everything we have is yours.
Alleluia!

A reading from the Good News given to us by Matthew.
Glory to you, Lord.

Jesus told his friends this story:
'There once was a rich man who owned a great deal of land. One day, he decided to plant a vineyard. He put up a fence, built a wine press, and built a tower.
When it was finished, he had to go abroad on a long journey, so he

DISCUSSION

Have the children retell the story in their own words.

Then move on to asking who the story is really about:
- God the Father, sending Jesus, his only son, to us.

When is it that we behave like the vineyard men?

And what will the owner (God the Father) do?

SHARING

Encourage the children to give examples of the splendours of creation.
What do they think is the most wonderful, the most beautiful? People, too, are part of creation. In what ways are they wonderful?

Look at the grapes in the bunch. They have grown on the same vine, and all had the same care. Are they all alike? Some are big, some small; some soft, some hard; some are good, some are bad, shrivelled.

What sort of grapes are we? What sort of grapes do we want to be? Jesus wants all of us to be the very best grapes possible.

rented the vineyard to some other men.
Some time later, after the grapes had grown fat, been gathered in, crushed and made into wine, the rich man sent his servants to collect his share of the wine from the men renting the vineyard. But they refused to pay up. They captured the servants, beat them up, and even killed one of them. The rich man sent more servants, and the same happened to them. Then he had an idea. "I'll send my only son", he said, "because they will respect him." When the men at the vineyard saw the son coming they made a plot to kill him. "If we kill him", the vineyard men said, "the vineyard will be ours." And they killed the man's only son.
Now what do you think the owner will do to those men?'
This is the Gospel of the Lord.
Praise to you, Lord Jesus Christ.

ACTIVITIES

> Have the children act out the Gospel story, making up their own ending.

> Have the children act out the story, substituting modern day equivalents of vineyard, etc.

> Give out the cut-outs.

> Have the children write or draw a prayer on them, thanking God for all he has given them; asking help to grow more like Jesus.

> Collect the grape shapes together to form a bunch.

THE HONOUR OF YOUR PRESENCE IS REQUESTED IN THE KINGDOM

VISUAL AIDS

> Pictures of weddings, first communion.

> Wedding cards and invitations.

> Picture of the Last Supper.

> Blank invitation cards.

WELCOME AND PROCLAIM THE GOSPEL

Say/sing together:

Alleluia, alleluia!
Lord, you have prepared
a banquet for us.
Alleluia!

A reading from the Good News given to us by Matthew.
Glory to you, Lord.

Jesus says,
'The kingdom of heaven is like a king who prepared a wonderful party for his son's wedding. On the wedding day the king sent his servants to call the invited guests.
But the invited guests refused to come. The king sent more servants to

DISCUSSION

Why was there a banquet?
- for the son's wedding.
Why did the invited guests not come?
What happened to the servants?
Unpack who the story characters really are:
- the king is God the Father;
- the servants are the prophets;
- we are the guests.

Where is the banquet, the banquet table?
- church and altar.
What is the feast?
- the celebration of the eucharist.
Focus on the invitation to communion: '. . . happy are those who are called to his supper'.

We are called to the Lord's supper; how do we respond?

SHARING

Encourage the children to share memories of celebrations they have enjoyed.
To be invited to a celebration is to share in a new or important stage in someone's life (birthday, wedding, etc.). Have the children give examples.

Celebrations need a great deal of preparation. Have the children give examples of what might need to be done.

Look at the Last Supper picture, and talk about sharing the Lord's table e.g. those who have made their first communion share their memories.

tell them everything was ready, and to come at once. But still the guests refused. One was too busy with his farm, another too busy with his business. Others beat up the king's servants, and killed them.
The king was furious. He sent in his army to destroy the murderers and to burn their town. But still there were no guests, so the king said to his servants "Go out to the streets and invite anyone you meet to come to the wedding." And so they did, and soon the wedding hall was filled with guests.'

This is the Gospel of the Lord.
Praise to you, Lord Jesus Christ.

ACTIVITIES

> Give each child a blank invitation card.

> Have them fill the card in:

....
(their own name)
The honour of your presence
is requested
in the kingdom of God.

> The children could decorate the cards, and then place them round the picture of the Last Supper.

GIVE TO GOD WHAT IS HIS

VISUAL AIDS

> Coins from different countries, preferably showing the heads of rulers.

WELCOME AND PROCLAIM THE GOSPEL

Say/sing together:

Alleluia, alleluia!
Praise to God our Father
for the many gifts he gives us.
Alleluia!

A reading from the Good News given to us by Matthew.
Glory to you, Lord.

One day some people came to Jesus to try and trick him.
'We know you are an honest man', they said, 'and that you always speak the truth. We know you're not afraid of anyone. So please tell us, is it right that we who are Jews should have to pay taxes to Caesar, the Roman

DISCUSSION

Show the coins, and ask why they have the heads of the rulers on them.
What was Jesus' first reply in today's story?
What do you think he meant?
- do not make the ruler of your country an excuse for not serving God.
Are we sometimes selfish? Keeping things to ourselves?

All our gifts come from God and remind us that we are made in the image of God.
Just as the coins bear the image of the country's ruler, we are like coins which bear the image of our ruler, who is God.
Made in the image of God, we should obey God, do what he wants of us.
As Jesus says in today's story: 'give to God what is his'.

SHARING

(If you have a really large group, it would be better to split into small groups.)
Invite each child to say what their name is, and to say something about themselves. Help them to say something which distinguishes them from the others:
e.g. is it possible to be mistaken for someone else?

Would your parents notice if they took someone else home instead of you? Would you notice if different parents took you home?

Each of us is different; each of us is special.

We have each been given special gifts by God, and all that he wants in return is that we use those gifts to give him glory and praise.

ruler?'
Jesus knew they were trying to trick him, so he said,
'Show me the money you use for the taxes.' They gave Jesus a coin.
'Whose head is this on the coin? Whose name?' he asked them.
'Caesar's', they replied.
'Very well then', said Jesus, 'give back to Caesar what is Caesar's, and give to God what belongs to God.'

This is the Gospel of the Lord.
Praise to you, Lord Jesus Christ.

ACTIVITIES

> Give out blank pieces of paper on which the children write or draw their personal gifts, and how they will use them in the week ahead to serve God, e.g.
> - by helping others;
> - by trying hard at school;
> - playing with/looking after a younger child.

I LOVE YOU

VISUAL AIDS

> Pictures of a castle, of Moses with the Ten Commandments, of people helping others.

> Heart shape cut-outs.

WELCOME AND PROCLAIM THE GOSPEL

Say/sing together:

Alleluia, alleluia!
Fill our hearts, Lord,
with your love.
Alleluia!

A reading from the Good News given to us by Matthew.
Glory to you, Lord.

Some people came to Jesus to try and trick him with this question,
'Of all the commandments, which one is the greatest?'
Jesus replied,
'You must love the Lord your God with all your heart, with all your soul, and with all your mind. This is

DISCUSSION

What was the trick?
- to try and get Jesus to say one commandment was more important than another.

What did Jesus say?
- that we should keep all the commandments.

How?
- if we love God we will put him first;
- if we love others we will do nothing to harm or upset them.

SHARING

Encourage the children to talk about the people they love most.
Who are they? Why do they love them?
Do they love strangers?

How do we show that we love someone?
When is it difficult to love?

To love, we must be strong.
God's love for us is strong, as strong as a castle or fortress that nothing can destroy.

In today's Gospel, Jesus tells us how to be strong in love.

the first and the greatest commandment. And the second commandment is like it: you must love your neighbour as yourself.'

This is the Gospel of the Lord.
Praise to you, Lord Jesus Christ.

ACTIVITIES

The commandments God gave to Moses were written on stone, but they should be written on our hearts.

> Give out the heart shape cut-outs.

> Have the children write or draw on them how they want the love of God to fill their hearts, and how they will be extra loving to

someone in the coming week.

BE A GOSPEL

VISUAL AIDS

> Pictures of pop stars, TV personalities, the Pope, Mother Teresa, Jesus.

> Tassels and tassel shape cut-outs.

WELCOME AND PROCLAIM THE GOSPEL

Say/sing together:

Alleluia, alleluia!
The greatest amongst
you must be your servant.
Alleluia!

A reading from the Good News given to us by Matthew.
Glory to you, Lord.

Jesus said to the people and to his friends,
'You must listen to the Scribes and Pharisees, and do what they tell you, because they are the teachers who tell us what the Ten Commandments mean. But do not do what the Scribes and Pharisees do, because they do

DISCUSSION

Who wore tassels?
- Scribes and Pharisees.

What did Jesus say about them?

Why did Jesus say not to imitate their behaviour?
- because they did not practise what they preached.
- they sought their own honour, not

God's.

How does Jesus ask us to live?
- as one family, loving and serving each other.

SHARING

Show the children the pictures and encourage them to discuss why various people are famous or important.

Do the children want to be famous? What do people wear to show that they are important, or that they have special work to do?
- crowns, medals, uniforms.

Sometimes people dress up to show off: get the children to give examples.

In today's Gospel we hear about some show offs.

not practise what they preach. Everything they do is to attract attention to themselves and make themselves important. They wear bigger and bigger tassels, and always like to sit at the best place at banquets. They take the front seats in the synagogue, so that people will be able to see them praying. And they love to be called "teacher".
You are all the one family of God our Father in heaven, so call no one on earth "master" or "teacher". Rather, love and serve each other.'

This is the Gospel of the Lord.
Praise to you, Lord Jesus Christ.

ACTIVITIES

> Mime the Gospel story, if possibly substituting present day equivalents.

> Give out the tassel shape cut-outs.

> Have the children write or draw on them ways in which they can behave more like Jesus.

32nd SUNDAY IN ORDINARY TIME

HE IS HERE

VISUAL AIDS

> Pictures of weddings.

> Two torches, one with batteries, one without.

> Lamp shape cut-outs.

WELCOME AND PROCLAIM THE GOSPEL

Say/sing together:

Alleluia, alleluia!
Receive the light of Christ.
Keep it burning brightly.
Alleluia!

A reading from the Good News given to us by Matthew.
Glory to you, Lord.

Jesus said:
'The kingdom of heaven is like this. Ten bridesmaids took their lamps and went out to meet the bridegroom. Five of the bridesmaids took extra oil with them, but the other five took only their lamps.
The bridegroom was late, very late.

DISCUSSION

A lamp without oil is like torches without batteries.
Show the torches.

The bridesmaids had been chosen for an important task:
what was it?
why did they need their lamps?

When we were baptised we too were given a light and asked to keep it burning brightly.
How do we keep the light of Christ burning brightly in our lives?
How might we let the light go out?

Play soft music, during which the children can pray quietly for the strength never to get tired of waiting for Jesus.

SHARING

Encourage the children to share their memories and experiences of preparing for a wedding, or some other big event.

Share experiences of meeting people. Talk about the preparations that are needed:
- meeting place, time, delays, waiting, transport, etc.

As it grew darker, the bridesmaids fell asleep. At midnight someone called out
"The bridegroom is here! Go out to meet him!" By now the bridesmaids' lamps had run out of oil. The five wise bridesmaids fixed their lamps with the spare oil they had brought. The five foolish bridesmaids asked the others for some of their spare oil. But they replied

"No, because we wouldn't have enough to light the way for the bridegroom. Go and buy some for yourselves." The five foolish ones went off to buy more oil, but while they were away, the bridegroom arrived. The wise bridesmaids went with him to the wedding, but the foolish ones missed it.'

This is the Gospel of the Lord.
Praise to you, Lord Jesus Christ.

ACTIVITIES

> Give out the lamp shape cut-outs.

> On them have the children write or draw:
   how they will wait for Jesus in the coming week;
   or how he might come into their lives each day;
   or how they will be ready to welcome him.

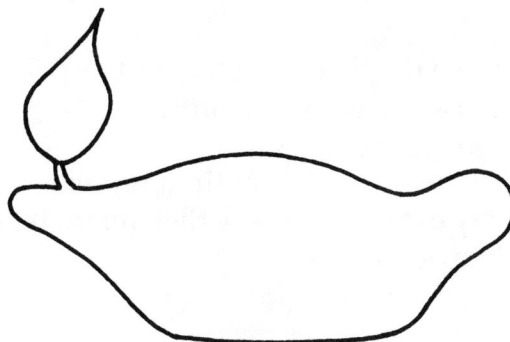

GLORY TO GOD

VISUAL AIDS

> A variety of gift-wrapped packages with blank labels.

> Pictures of children doing different things, e.g. playing music, writing, building, swimming, etc.

> Blank label shape cut-outs.

WELCOME AND PROCLAIM THE GOSPEL

Say/sing together:

**Alleluia, alleluia!
Well done, good and faithful
    servant.
Come and join God's happiness.
Alleluia!**

A reading from the Good News given to us by Matthew.
Glory to you, Lord.

Jesus said:
'Once there was a rich man, who had to go on a long journey, so he called his servants, and asked them to look after his business while he was away. To one he gave five talents; to another, two talents; to a third, one talent. Then he set out. The first

DISCUSSION

Have the children retell the Gospel story in their own words.

Discuss with the children present day examples of how they might be like the three servants.

SHARING

Encourage the children to talk about the 'gifts' that the children in the pictures are using:
- arms, legs, ears, voices, etc.
How many gifts have we used this morning?

On the package labels write the names of the gifts that the children identify.

God gives us these gifts; how do we share them with others?
Do we share them at home? at school? at play?

Have the children identify the gift they most appreciate.
Let us praise and thank God for our gifts.
Sing or say the Gloria.

servant with five talents went out and traded with them and earned five more. The servant with two talents used them to make two more. The servant with one talent dug a hole and hid it. After a long time, the master returned, and called his servants to know what they had done with the talents. The servant who had five showed him the ten he now had; the next showed him his two extra. "Well done, good and faithful servants. Because you can be trusted with these small things, I will trust you with greater. Come and share the happiness of my house." Then along came the servant with only one talent. When the master heard how it had been hidden in the ground, he was angry. He took the talent away from the lazy servant, and had him thrown into prison.'
This is the Gospel of the Lord.
Praise to you, Lord Jesus Christ.

ACTIVITIES

> Have the children mime the Gospel, preferably with present day interpretation.

> Give out blank label cut-outs, and have the children write or draw how they will use one of their gifts in the coming week.

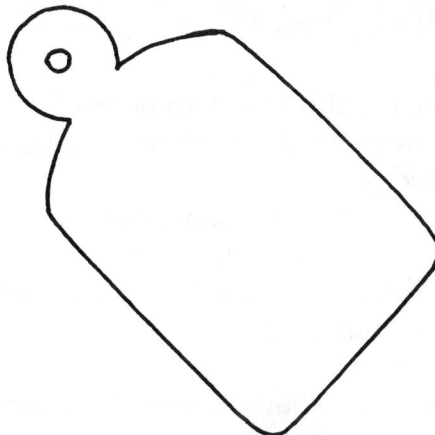

WELCOME TO MY KINGDOM

VISUAL AIDS

> Pictures of Jesus:
  as the Good Shepherd,
  with children,
  healing,
  in triumph on the cross.

> Crown or cross shape cut-outs.

WELCOME AND PROCLAIM THE GOSPEL

Say/sing together:

**Alleluia, alleluia!
Blessed is he who comes
in the name of the Lord!
Alleluia!**

A reading from the Good News given to us by Matthew.
Glory to you, Lord.

Jesus says,
'Who are the people that my Father will welcome into the Kingdom? The Kingdom will be full of the people who gave me food when I was hungry;
who gave me drink when I was thirsty;

DISCUSSION

Who are the Kingdom people?
- those who are mentioned by Jesus in today's Gospel;
- those who need food, clothing, etc.

Who are the people today who need these things?
- hungry
- strangers (new children in school or neighbourhood)

- imprisoned (housebound)

Jesus' Kingdom is built with love in the lives of people.
How can we be Kingdom builders in the week ahead?
Have the children choose one example and say what they might do.

SHARING

Today we celebrate the honour of having Jesus as our King.

Encourage the children to say what they know about kings (or queens); if they were King/Queen for a day, what would they do?

What kind of King is Jesus?
- he is King of love, truth, peace, justice, etc.
- he is the Good Shepherd who carries his lambs home to safety on his shoulders.

The whole world is Jesus' kingdom, but only if we want him as our King, only if we let him rule over us, only if we let him be the King of our lives. Jesus tells us what it will be like if we let him rule our lives.

who made me welcome when I was a stranger;
who clothed me when I was naked;
who visited me when I was sick;
who came to see me when I was in prison.
These are the people my Father will welcome into the Kingdom.
Whatever you do to the least of these my friends, you do to me.'
This is the Gospel of the Lord.
Praise to you, Lord Jesus Christ.

ACTIVITIES

> Give out the cut-out shapes.

> On them have the children write or draw:

either, how they can spread the Kingdom of love in the week ahead;

or, how they can use the power of Jesus to conquer what is not love, e.g. selfishness, tale-telling, laziness, lies, etc.

> Have the children make a card that they can send to someone who is sick, lonely, in prison (e.g. through Amnesty International).

WHERE DO YOU LIVE, JESUS?

VISUAL AIDS

> Pictures of houses from different parts of the world.

> A variety of house shape cut-outs.

WELCOME AND PROCLAIM THE GOSPEL

Say/sing together:

**Alleluia, alleluia!
Lord, come
and make your home with us.
Alleluia!**

A reading from the Good News given to us by John.
Glory to you, Lord.

John the Baptist and two of his friends were standing together when Jesus passed by.
'Look', said John, 'there is the lamb of God.'
When John's friends heard this they set off to follow Jesus. When Jesus saw them, he asked them,

DISCUSSION

Has anyone asked the children where they lived?
Have the children ever asked anyone where they live?

Have they ever been invited to anyone else's home?
Or have they invited anyone to theirs?

Do you think John's friends enjoyed their visit with Jesus?
What might they have talked about together?

What might you talk to Jesus about if you visited him or he visited you?

SHARING

Encourage the children to talk about where they live;
their neighbourhood, the type of house;
other people's homes they have visited.

What are reasons for visiting people?
Where do they like to visit?

Who visits them at home? How do they welcome visitors?

In today's Gospel we hear what happens when two friends of John the Baptist go to visit Jesus.

'What do you want?'
'We want to know where you live', they replied.
'Come and see', said Jesus.
They went with Jesus, saw where he lived, and stayed with him for the rest of the day.

This is the Gospel of the Lord.
Praise to you, Lord Jesus Christ.

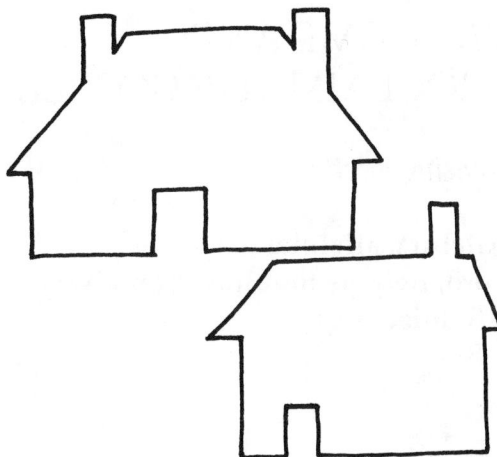

ACTIVITIES

At Mass every Sunday we visit with Jesus; we hear him speak to us in the Gospel.

By visiting him every week we should come to know him better and become his friends.

> Have the children mime the Gospel story, adding what they imagine happened during the disciples' visit with Jesus.

> Give out the house shape cut-outs.

> Have the children write or draw a thank you to Jesus for inviting them to his house each week.

FOLLOW ME

VISUAL AIDS

> Pictures of fishermen, nets and boats.

> Pictures of people who follow Jesus now.

WELCOME AND PROCLAIM THE GOSPEL

Say/sing together:

Alleluia, alleluia!
Lord, help us to follow you always.
Alleluia!

A reading from the Good News given to us by Mark.
Glory to you, Lord.

As he was walking by the sea of Galilee Jesus saw two men fishing. It was Simon and his brother Andrew. Jesus called to them,
'Follow me, and I will make you into fishers of man.'
At once they left their nets and followed him.

DISCUSSION

Where was Jesus?
Who did he see first?
What did Jesus call to them?
What did they do?
Then who did Jesus see?
What were they doing?
What did they do when Jesus called them?

How do the children respond when they are called?
- for dinner?
- from play?
- to help?
- for bed?
Who are the people that call them?

What does Jesus call them to do?

SHARING

Have the children play the game of 'follow the leader'. After a time, encourage the leader to mime actions to do with fishing.

Then encourage the children to talk about the game:
sometimes it is easy to follow the leader, sometimes it is hard.

We want to follow Jesus:
- when is it hard?
- when is it easy?

In today's Gospel we hear about some men who Jesus invited to follow him.

Further along the shore, they met some more fishermen. It was the brothers James and John, helping their father to mend the nets.
'Follow me', called Jesus.
At once James and John set off to follow him.

This is the Gospel of the Lord.
Praise to you, Lord Jesus Christ.

ACTIVITIES

> Have the children mime the Gospel.

> Have the children mime the ways they are called in their own lives.

> Give out blank paper and have the children draw a picture of someone who is a good follower of Jesus today.

JESUS IS LORD

VISUAL AIDS

> Pictures of the risen Jesus, and of the cross.

> Card to make badges.

WELCOME AND PROCLAIM THE GOSPEL

Say/sing together:

**Alleluia, alleluia!
Jesus reveals the power of God.
Listen to his word.
Alleluia!**

A reading from the Good News given to us by Mark.
Glory to you, Lord.

One day, as Jesus was teaching in the synagogue, a man filled with an evil spirit came in and shouted,
'What do you want with us, Jesus of Nazareth? Have you come to destroy us? I know who you are, you are the Holy One of God!'
'Be quiet!' said Jesus, 'Come out of

DISCUSSION

Where was Jesus?
- in the synagogue.
What was Jesus doing?
- teaching.
What happened?
- a man started shouting at Jesus.
Why did the man shout like this?
- because he was full of an evil spirit.

How did Jesus use his power?
- to heal the man, to get rid of the evil spirit.
How can he use his power in our lives?
- to help us overcome selfishness, greed, etc.

SHARING

Encourage the children to give examples of difficult tasks they have accomplished.

What was the hardest thing they ever did?

Can they think of examples of difficult things that other people do?

Sometimes one thing we find very hard is to love each other. Some times it's easier to quarrel, fight, refuse to share.

But Jesus has great power. He can help us to face these difficult tasks. He has the power to change us. His power helps us love others. His power can help us to change the whole world.

him!'
Immediately the evil spirit came out of the man. The people were amazed and said to each other 'Who is this man who has such power over evil?'

This is the Gospel of the Lord.
Praise to you, Lord Jesus Christ.

ACTIVITIES

> Have the children make a JESUS IS LORD badge.

JESUS IS LORD

> Recite the following prayer together, the children repeating it line by line:

**Jesus,
be the Lord of our lives.
Help us spread your goodness
everywhere we go.**

TIME FOR JESUS

VISUAL AIDS

> Pictures of people engaged in everyday activities.

> A clock.

> Cards with clock faces on them (one for each child).

WELCOME AND PROCLAIM THE GOSPEL

Say/sing together:

**Alleluia, alleluia!
Jesus takes our sickness away.
Alleluia!**

A reading from the Good News given to us by Mark.
Glory to you, Lord.

Jesus left the synagogue where he had been teaching and went with his friends to Simon's house. There they found that Simon's mother-in-law was sick with a fever. Jesus went to her, took her by the hand and helped her up. She recovered immediately. Later, people of the town began to

DISCUSSION

How did Jesus spend his day?

When and where did he like to pray?

Where and when do you pray?

Do you have a special place?

A favourite prayer?

ACTIVITIES

> Give out the clock faces.

> Have the children divide up the clock face to represent what they do with their time. Have them colour in the amount of time they will give to Jesus in prayer in the week ahead.

SHARING

Have the children ever heard adults say 'I wish I had more time...'?
Why do people want more time?

What will they do with the time?

Does anyone ever say 'I wish I had more time for Jesus', or 'I wish I had more time for prayer'?

Talk about morning and night prayers; about praying in church; and not disturbing others who are praying.

Let us listen now to today's Gospel, when we will hear how Jesus spent his day, and what happened.

---

bring all the sick people. Soon there were great crowds around the house. Jesus cured many of the sick and suffering.

Next morning, before dawn, Jesus got up, and went away to find a quiet place where he could be by himself to pray.
Later, Simon and the others came looking for him.
'Everyone wants you', they told him.

So they began to travel around all the towns, where Jesus preached to the people.

This is the Gospel of the Lord.
Praise to you, Lord Jesus Christ.

> Recite this prayer together:

**Loving Father,
watch over us and our families.
Keep us always safe in your care.**

6th SUNDAY IN ORDINARY TIME

JESUS, TOUCH MY HEART WITH LOVE

VISUAL AIDS

> Pictures of happy people.

> A selection of flowers, some in tight bud, some open.

> Flower shape cut-outs.

WELCOME AND PROCLAIM THE GOSPEL

Say/sing together:

Alleluia, alleluia!
Jesus saves us
and we are full of joy.
Alleluia!

A reading from the Good News given to us by Mark.
Glory to you, Lord.

One day a leper came to Jesus, knelt at his feet and begged for help. Jesus felt sorry for the leper, stretched out his hand and touched him. At once the man was cured.
Jesus said to him
'Don't tell anyone, but go and show yourself to the priest.'

DISCUSSION

Do the children know what leprosy is?
- a terrible skin disease. Because there was no cure for it in Jesus' time, people were very afraid of anyone with leprosy.

To prevent the disease spreading, lepers had to live outside the town. They were outcasts.

What did Jesus do for the leper?
What did Jesus ask him to do?
- not to tell anyone, to keep it a secret.
What did the leper do?
- because he was so happy, he couldn't keep it a secret!
So what was the result?
What happened to Jesus?

SHARING

Invite the children to look at the flowers. Help the children notice that some are closed, some are open. Sometimes the buds never open.

People can be like the flowers:
some are bright, cheery, and friendly;
others are mean, selfish and tightly closed on themselves.

Encourage the children to give examples of 'open' and 'closed' people.

Jesus' love in our hearts helps us to open up, to grow into being friendly people, who share what we have with others, making the world a happy place.

But the man went off and told everyone what had happened to him, spreading the news far and wide. This meant Jesus could no longer go into the towns, but had to stay outside. Even so, people came to him from all around.

This is the Gospel of the Lord.
Praise to you, Lord Jesus Christ.

ACTIVITIES

> Give out the flower shape cut-outs.

> In the centre of the shapes, have the children write
'FILL MY HEART WITH LOVE';
on the petals have them write or draw the ways in which they want Jesus to change their lives.

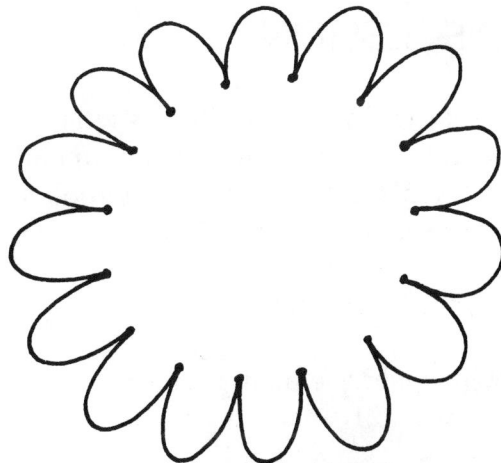

FRIEND-SHIP IS . . .

VISUAL AIDS

> Pictures of friends, happy together, helping each other out.

> Hand shape cut-outs.

WELCOME AND PROCLAIM THE GOSPEL

Say/sing together:

Alleluia, alleluia!
Lord, increase our faith.
Alleluia!

A reading from the Good News given to us by Mark.
Glory to you, Lord.

Jesus came back to the town of Capernaum. When the news got around, so many people came to see and listen to him that the house where he was staying was soon full to overflowing.
Four men came along, bringing their friend on a stretcher. Their friend

DISCUSSION

Lead the children to discuss what good friends the paralysed man had; the great deal of trouble they took to help him.

What did they do?

Why could the man not help himself?

How were their efforts rewarded?

Do the children know anyone needing help?

Encourage the children to give examples of things that some people cannot do for themselves, for which they need help.

SHARING

Encourage the children to name their friends.

What is it about these people that they like, that makes them friends?

Friends share happy times with us, and stand by us in bad ones.

was paralysed, and could not do anything for himself. His friends hoped that Jesus would heal him. But the crowd around Jesus was so great that they could not even get near the door.
So they climbed up on to the flat roof of the house, made a hole in it, and lowered their friend on the stretcher down through the hole.
Seeing their faith, Jesus said to the man

'Your sins are forgiven. Get up, pick up your bed and go home.'
At once the man got up, picked up his bed and walked out in front of everyone. Everyone was astonished.

This is the Gospel of the Lord.
Praise to you, Lord Jesus Christ.

ACTIVITIES

> Have the children mime the Gospel story.

> Give out the hand shape cut-outs.

> Have the children write or draw on the hand shape how they will give someone a helping hand during the coming week.

> Recite the following prayer together, the children repeating it line by line:
**Lord,
give us faith
in your power to heal.
Give us friends
when we are in need.
Help us to be good friends
to others when they are in need.**

REJOICE! JESUS IS HERE!

VISUAL AIDS

> Pictures of weddings.

> Patched garments.

> If possible, a wineskin (e.g. as sold as souvenirs of Spain).

> Heart shape cut-outs.

WELCOME AND PROCLAIM THE GOSPEL

Say/sing together:

Alleluia, alleluia!
Fill us with your love, Lord.
Alleluia!

A reading from the Good News given to us by Mark.
Glory to you, Lord.

One day, John the Baptist, his followers and the Pharisees were fasting. Jesus and his friends were not. The people wanted to know why not.
This is how Jesus answered:
'Nobody would dream of fasting at a wedding while the bridegroom is

DISCUSSION

Who was fasting? Who was not?
Who is the bridegroom?
- Jesus. His friends are full of joy when he is with them.
A riddle: what do these have in common
- a wedding?
- the patched garment?
- the wineskins?
They are all about newness.

- a wedding is the beginning of a new married life;
- old and new cloth do not go together, all must be new;
- new wine needs new skins.

Jesus wants us to live the new life he has come to give us. It is not enough to patch up our old life. Our hearts must be like new wineskins filled with the good new wine of Jesus' love.

SHARING

Using the pictures, encourage the children to share their memories and experiences of weddings.

Ask the children to look at the patched garment.
Why are clothes patched?
What kind of material is used for patches?

What might happen if an old coat is patched with new material?
- the old would wear out faster than the new, which would tear away.

Show the children the wineskin; explain that bottles were too rare and expensive.

Today's Gospel is about weddings, patching old clothes, and wineskins.

---

still there. After he leaves, they might fast.
To fast at a wedding would be as strange as repairing an old cloak with new material. Everyone knows the patch would tear away, and the cloak would have an even worse tear.
To fast at a wedding would be as strange as putting new wine into old wineskins, which would burst and spill the wine. Everyone knows that

new wine should go into new wineskins.'

This is the Gospel of the Lord.
Praise to you, Lord Jesus Christ.

ACTIVITIES

> Give out the heart shape cut-outs.

> Have the children write or draw on them something new they will do in the coming week;
ways in which they can spread the joy of Jesus;
ways they can be happy during the week.

> Lead the children in this prayer:
Let us pray
that the Lord will help us
to make life full of joy
for those we meet this week.
Lord, hear us.
Lord, graciously hear us.
Let us pray
that the Lord will fill our hearts
with the message of your Gospel.
Lord, hear us.
Lord, graciously hear us.

LORD, FILL OUR HEARTS WITH LOVE

VISUAL AIDS

> Ears of wheat, a loaf of bread.

> Heart shape cut-outs.

WELCOME AND PROCLAIM THE GOSPEL

Say/sing together:

**Alleluia, alleluia!
Lord, you have the message
of eternal life.
Alleluia!**

A reading from the Good News given to us by Mark.
Glory to you, Lord.

One sabbath day Jesus and his friends were walking through the cornfields. They were hungry; so as they walked along some of them began to pick ears of corn, and eat them. When the Pharisees saw this they complained to Jesus, 'Your friends are breaking the

DISCUSSION

What were the friends of Jesus doing?
Give out the ears of corn for the children to rub.
Is there much to eat in the ears?
Get the children to notice how much fuss the Pharisees were making about something so little.
What did King David and his men do?

They ate bread. Get the children to compare the size of the loaf with the ears of corn; there are many grains in the bread.
Why did they take the bread?
Because they were starving.

Jesus is telling us that people are more important than laws.

SHARING

Which are more important: people or rules?
Encourage the children to give examples of rules and laws.
Why do we have rules and laws?
- to protect people.
Get the children to give examples of how laws and rules protect them
- e.g. Highway Code of rules to prevent accidents.

God has made some wonderful laws:
that we should have night and day;
that the stars stay in the sky;
that the sun shines;
that the rain falls; that plants grow;
that we can hear, see, speak . . .

Say/sing a Gloria together to thank and praise God for his wonderful laws.

sabbath law by picking corn today.'
Jesus replied
'Have you never heard what King David and his friends did when they were hungry? They went into the Temple and ate the loaves of offering which only the priests are allowed to eat.'
Jesus then went into the synagogue, where a man with a withered hand came to him. The Pharisees were still watching Jesus, so he asked them,

'Is it against the law to do a good deed on the sabbath day?' They could not reply. Jesus cured the man's hand, which made the Pharisees even more furious.

This is the Gospel of the Lord.
Praise to you, Lord Jesus Christ.

ACTIVITIES

What did Jesus do in the synagogue?
What is the one law that Jesus gave us that we must never break?
- the law of love, that we should love one another.

> Give out the heart shape cut-outs.

> Have the children write or draw on them how they will keep Jesus' law of love with all their heart in the week ahead.

THIS IS MY FAMILY

VISUAL AIDS

> Pictures of families, including the Holy Family.

> People shape cut-outs.

WELCOME AND PROCLAIM THE GOSPEL

Say/sing together:

Alleluia, alleluia!
Anyone who does God's will
is my brother and sister and mother.
Alleluia!

A reading from the Good News given to us by Mark.
Praise to you, Lord Jesus Christ.

Jesus went with his disciples to Nazareth, the town where he had grown up, and where his mother still lived. When they arrived, such a crowd came to see Jesus that they could not even have a meal.
When Jesus' relatives heard what was happening, they were worried

DISCUSSION

What happens in today's Gospel story?
What did Jesus' family think?
- they were worried about him.

What were they going to do?
- take him home again.

If Jesus went home, would he have been able to preach, teach and heal?

What did Jesus say about his family?
- Jesus' family is anyone who shows they are a child of God the Father.

How do we show we are children of God our Father?
- by doing God's will, by living God's way of love.
Encourage the children to give examples.

SHARING

What does it mean to belong to a family?
What is a family?
- mother, father, brothers, sisters, grandparents, aunts, uncles, cousins, etc.
Who belonged to Jesus' family?
- Mary, Joseph, John the Baptist, Zachary, Elizabeth, etc.

about him, and came to see if they could help. They wanted to take him home again.
Meantime, some Scribes who had come from Jerusalem were saying that Jesus was a friend of the devil. Jesus proved how foolish such talk was.
'You can see that the devil is being chased from many people. Would this happen if the devil were helping me? Can the devil fight himself? No!'

A messenger came to tell Jesus his family had arrived and were outside waiting for him. Jesus said, 'Anyone who believes in me and does the will of my Father is my brother and sister and mother.'

This is the Gospel of the Lord.
Praise to you, Lord Jesus Christ.

ACTIVITIES

> Give out the people shape cut-outs.

> Have the children write or draw on them how they can be a brother/sister to Jesus in the coming week.

THE KINGDOM OF GOD IS LIKE . . .

VISUAL AIDS

> Pictures of children from babyhood through to teenage.

> Some baby clothes or shoes.

> Seeds or peas or beans in various stages of growth.

> Seed shape cut-outs.

WELCOME AND PROCLAIM THE GOSPEL

Say/sing together:

**Alleluia, alleluia!
May the seed of God's word
grow strong in our hearts.
Alleluia!**

A reading from the Good News given to us by Mark.
Glory to you, Lord.

Jesus told this story:
'One day a farmer went out, planted seeds in his fields, and then went home.
While he slept at night and while he worked during the day, the seeds under the ground were sprouting and growing, until one day when

DISCUSSION

What happened to the farmer's field?
Why do you think Jesus says the kingdom of God is like seeds?
- because they have the power to grow.
How are we like the seeds?
- because we too have the power to grow, and help God's kingdom.
What is the power of God in us?
- love.

ACTIVITIES

> Give out the seed shape cut-outs.

> Have the children write or draw on them how they want to grow into a loving person.

> Here is a poem about trees that have grown tall and strong. Good people are like the trees. Act out

SHARING

Show the children the seeds and plants, and encourage them to talk about growing and changing.

Show the pictures of children, and encourage the children to talk about how they have changed since birth. Use the clothes or shoes to demonstrate how they have grown.

Do we ever see anything or anyone growing?

In today's Gospel Jesus tells us a story about a farmer and his seeds, and what happened on his farm.

the farmer went back to his field, it was full of crops.
The farmer hadn't seen the seeds sprout and grow, and he didn't understand how they grew, but they grew nevertheless.'
Then Jesus said,
'That is what God's kingdom is like. Even the tiniest of seeds can grow to become the biggest of trees, big enough for all the birds to make their nests in its branches.'

This is the Gospel of the Lord.
Praise to you, Lord Jesus Christ.

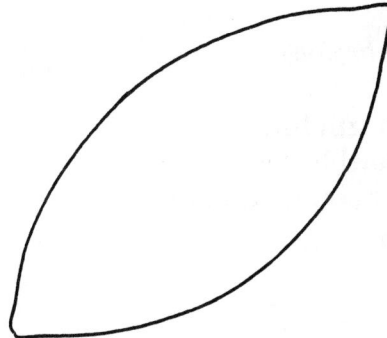

the response as well as saying it after each of the three verses:
Response:
The good will flourish like the palm tree
(arms above head, sway from side to side)
and grow tall like the cedar tree.
(stretch tall and straight)

With your roots in the house of the Lord

you will grow strong in the courts of our God.
Response

You will still give fruit when you are old,
and your leaves will still be green.
Response

Give thanks to the Lord our God and proclaim that the Lord is just.
Response

HAVE FAITH

VISUAL AIDS

> Pictures of sea and ships.

> Boat shape cut-outs.

WELCOME AND PROCLAIM THE GOSPEL

Say/sing together:

**Alleluia, alleluia!
Truly Lord Jesus,
you are the Son of God.
Alleluia!**

A reading from the Good News given to us by Mark.
Glory to you, Lord.

One evening, after a day of speaking to the crowds, Jesus said to his friends,
'Let us get into boats and cross over to the far side of the lake.'
So Jesus and his friends set sail, and other boats followed them.
Suddenly a great gale began to

DISCUSSION

What happened in the story?

Would you have been scared if you had been there?

Was Jesus scared?

What did Jesus say?

What things are the children scared of?

What makes us scared?
- things we cannot trust.

What do they think Jesus would say about these things that scare them.
- trust me.

SHARING

Encourage the children to share their experiences of the sea; sailing, or from TV programmes, films, stories, etc.

In today's Gospel we hear what happened when Jesus and some of his friends went sailing.

blow, and the waves became so huge that they came into the boat, almost sinking it.
Jesus' friends were terrified, but Jesus was fast asleep in the stern, with his head on a cushion. They woke him up, shouting 'We are sinking! We are sinking! Don't you care!'
Jesus woke up and said to the wind 'Be quiet!', and to the sea 'Be calm!'

The wind dropped, and all was calm again.
Jesus asked his friends
'Why were you so frightened? How is that that you didn't have faith?'
They were all amazed and said to each other 'Who is this man? Even the wind and sea obey him!'

This is the Gospel of the Lord.
Praise to you, Lord Jesus Christ.

ACTIVITIES

> Have the children mime the Gospel. Some can be Jesus and his friends, the rest can be the waves.

> Give out the boat shape cut-outs.

> Have the children make up and write out an act of faith: e.g.

'I believe that Jesus is my friend. He will never let me down.'

'I believe God my Father loves me, and will always take care of me.'

GOD LOVES YOU

VISUAL AIDS

> Pictures of Jesus.

> Pictures of happy children.

WELCOME AND PROCLAIM THE GOSPEL

Say/sing together:

**Alleluia, alleluia!
Lay your hands on us
and give us life, Lord.
Alleluia!**

A reading from the Good News given to us by Mark.
Glory to you, Lord.

Jesus was talking to a large crowd at the lakeside when an important man called Jairus came to him. He knelt at Jesus' feet and said
'My little girl is very sick. Please come and lay your hands on her to make her better and save her life.'
Jesus got up and followed Jairus

DISCUSSION

Who was Jairus?
What did he want from Jesus?
What did Jesus say to him?

What happened at Jairus' house?
Did everyone believe Jesus?

If you had been there, would you have laughed at Jesus when he said the girl was only sleeping?

What happened to the little girl?
How did her parents feel?

SHARING

Encourage the children to share memories of happy experiences.

What did it feel like?
What makes the children really happy?

What might be the worst thing they can imagine?

In today's Gospel we hear the story of Jesus and a little girl and the happiest thing in the world that happened to her. Listen carefully, because there will be questions afterwards.

towards his house, and many of the crowd followed them. When they were near the house some of Jairus' servants came running out to say 'Do not trouble Jesus. It's too late! Your little girl has died.'
Jesus heard them and said to Jairus 'Do not be afraid. Have faith.' Then to the family, who were all crying, Jesus said
'Why are you crying? The little girl is not dead - she is only sleeping.'

Jesus sent everyone out of the house except Jairus and his wife, and three of his friends. They all went into the girl's room. Jesus took her by the hand and said 'Little girl, get up.' Immediately the little girl got up and began to walk about. Her parents were astonished. Jesus told them not to tell anyone, and to give the girl something to eat.
This is the Gospel of the Lord.
Praise to you, Lord Jesus Christ.

ACTIVITIES

> Have the children act out the Gospel story. Those who do not have individual parts should be part of the crowd, and the girl's family.

> Have the children draw a picture of the story.

> Have the children write a thank you note to God for their health and happiness.

OUR FRIEND JESUS

VISUAL AIDS

> Picture or statue of Jesus.

WELCOME AND PROCLAIM THE GOSPEL

Say/sing together:

Alleluia, alleluia!
Lord, increase our faith.
Alleluia!

A reading from the Good News given to us by Mark.
Glory to you, Lord.

One sabbath day Jesus and his friends were visiting Nazareth, which is the town where Jesus had grown up. Everyone knew him and his family.
Since it was the sabbath they all went to the synagogue, where Jesus spoke to the people. They were

DISCUSSION

Ask the children how they feel about today's story.
If they had known Jesus ever since he had been a little boy, would they have been surprised when he started to work miracles?
Do you think the people of Nazareth were fair to Jesus?
Sometimes we can be unfair to people by having a fixed idea in our

heads of what they are like.
They might not be like that. If they were once, they might have changed.
Each week when we gather together to listen to the Good News of the Gospel, we begin with a special response. First of all we welcome the Gospel with the Alleluia (which means 'Praise the Lord'); then we hear the reader say 'A reading from the Good News . . .' to which we all

SHARING

Who is Jesus?
Encourage the children to share what they know about Jesus.
How might they find out more about him?
How do they become his friend?

Jesus is the best friend we could ever have, given to us by God our Father.

To thank God for the gift of Jesus' friendship say/sing a Gloria together.

In today's Gospel we will hear about people who thought they knew Jesus very well. Listen carefully, and see if you think they were friendly to him.

astonished by what Jesus said 'Where did he get all this knowledge and learning from? How can he work so many miracles? We've known him since he was a boy. We know his mother Mary and the rest of his family.'
They refused to believe in him and would not accept him. Jesus was amazed at their lack of faith, and could not work any miracles there.

This is the Gospel of the Lord.
Praise to you, Lord Jesus Christ.

respond 'Glory to you, Lord'. While we say this we should cross our forehead, lips and heart.
This is to show that we do want to listen to Jesus.
That we do believe him.
That we want his words to fill our minds, our hearts, and be on our lips.

Practise the actions and prayers with the children.

ACTIVITIES

> On a blank piece of paper, have the children write or draw:
how they will be a friend of Jesus;
how they will keep Jesus in their minds and hearts, and on their lips.

I LIVE!

VISUAL AIDS

> Pictures of apostles, missionaries.

> A rucksack, some money, anorak, sandals.

> People shape cut-outs.

WELCOME AND PROCLAIM THE GOSPEL

Say/sing together:

Alleluia, alleluia!
Lord, you have the message
of eternal life.
Alleluia!

A reading from the Good News given to us by Mark.
Glory to you, Lord.

Jesus called together his twelve special friends, and sent them out, two by two.
He told them to take nothing for the journey: no food; no haversack; no money in their wallets; not even a spare tunic; they were to wear sandals on their feet.

DISCUSSION

Who were Jesus' friends?

Why do you think Jesus sent them out two by two?

What did Jesus say they should not take?

Why do you think Jesus said not to take these things?

- so that they would be really free.

Wouldn't they need some of these things?
- not if they were staying with people who made them welcome.

What was to happen if they were not made welcome?

SHARING

What is the message Jesus brings us?
- love.
How is that message spread throughout the world?
What should people do when they hear the message of Jesus?
- turn away from their old life;
- start to live a life of love.

Saint Francis of Assisi was one person who listened to Jesus' message, and changed his life. This is called Saint Francis' prayer:
Lord Jesus, where there is hatred let me be loving; where there is hurt let me be forgiving; where there is fighting let me bring peace; where there is sadness let me bring comfort and joy.

Jesus said to them,
'Stay in any house where you are made welcome. If you're not made welcome, and if the people refuse to listen to you, walk away from them, and shake the dust from your feet.'

So they set out two by two, as Jesus instructed them, teaching and preaching, helping the people and healing the sick.

This is the Gospel of the Lord.
Praise to you, Lord Jesus Christ.

ACTIVITIES

> Divide into groups of two.

> The groups have to decide what they will do next week so that other people will say they are Good News.

> Write or draw on the people shape cut-outs what it is they have decided to do in the coming week.

LISTEN TO MY VOICE

VISUAL AIDS

> Pictures of people on holiday.

> Picture postcards.

> Holiday brochures (to cut up).

WELCOME AND PROCLAIM THE GOSPEL

Say/sing together:

Alleluia, alleluia!
Lord, be our leader;
teach us your way.
Alleluia!

A reading from the Good News given to us by Mark.
Glory to you, Lord.

The friends of Jesus who went out two by two now came back, and told Jesus all that they had said and done. Jesus told them they deserved a rest and a holiday.
He and his friends had been so busy they had not even time to eat. So they went off in a boat to a quiet

DISCUSSION

How were Jesus' friends when they came back?
- tired out from all their work.

What did Jesus say they should do?
- go away for a rest and a holiday.

What happened?
- the people guessed where they were going and got there first.

Was Jesus cross with the people who spoiled his holiday?
- no, he felt sorry for them.

What did Jesus do for the people who were waiting for him?
- he spent time speaking to them, and teaching them.

Are we like these people? Are we ready to listen to Jesus' teaching?

SHARING

Invite the children to look at the pictures.
Encourage them to share their memories of holidays.
Do they think holidays make people happy?
Jesus wants us to be happy.
He tells us that we will be happy if we listen to his voice.

Today we hear how Jesus and his friends plan to have a holiday - but what happens?

place for some rest.
But some people saw them leaving, and guessed where they were going. The word went round, so that by the time Jesus and his friends reached where they were going, there was already a crowd of people waiting for them.
When he saw the crowd Jesus was sorry for them, because they were like sheep without a shepherd. He took pity on them, and spent a long time speaking to them and teaching them.

This is the Gospel of the Lord.
Praise to you, Lord Jesus Christ.

ACTIVITIES

> Have the children act out the Gospel:
encourage them to make up the reports given by the apostles; and what they thought Jesus would have said to the apostles.

> Using pictures cut from the holiday brochures, have the children make up a holiday postcard.

> For the message on the postcard, have the children make up and write a prayer asking Jesus to help them listen to his voice.

17th SUNDAY IN ORDINARY TIME

JESUS FEEDS THE PEOPLE

VISUAL AIDS

> Picture/s of a crowd.

> Bread or bread rolls.

> Tin of sardines.

> Loaf or bread shape cut-outs.

WELCOME AND PROCLAIM THE GOSPEL

Say/sing together:

Alleluia, alleluia!
God has visited his people.
Alleluia!

A reading from the Good News given to us by John.
Glory to you, Lord.

A huge crowd had been listening to Jesus all day. The people would be tired and hungry. Jesus said to Philip 'Where can we buy some bread for the people to eat?'
Philip replied
'Two hundred silver coins would only buy enough to give them a

DISCUSSION

What sort of day had it been?
What did Jesus want to do?

What did Philip say?
What did Andrew suggest?
Did he think there was enough?

If you were the little boy, how would you feel?

What did Jesus do?
(Try to convey the simple fourfold structure of taking, blessing, breaking and sharing.)

What gifts have you got that you can share with others for Jesus?

SHARING

Invite the children to look at all the visual aids, and invite them to guess what today's Gospel story is about.

What do we have that we can share? Focus the discussion away from material things, to the children themselves, e. g.
I have hands to set tables . . .; I have legs to run messages . . ., etc.

Today's Gospel tells us about a little boy who shared
- what did he share?
- and who did he share it with?

small piece each.'
Then Andrew said,
'There's a small boy here who has five barley loaves and two fishes - but that won't feed this crowd!'
Jesus said
'Make the people sit down.'
When all the people, about five thousand, were sitting on the grass, Jesus took the loaves, gave thanks, and shared them with all who were ready. He then did the same with the fish.
When everyone had eaten enough Jesus asked his friends to pick up what was left over. The scraps they picked up filled twelve baskets. The people thought Jesus was wonderful and wanted to make him their king. But Jesus went away to the hills to be by himself.

This is the Gospel of the Lord.
Praise to you, Lord Jesus Christ.

ACTIVITIES

> Have the children mime the Gospel.

> Give out the cut-out shapes.

> On them have the children write or draw what it is that they will share in the coming week.

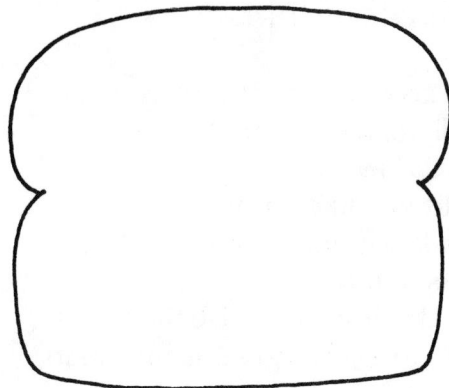

I AM THE BREAD OF LIFE

VISUAL AIDS
> Pictures of a desert.
> Plate or card covered in gold paper.
> Bread or bread rolls.
> Loaf or bread shape cut-outs.

SHARING
Today we have two stories. The second one will be the Gospel story of Jesus as usual; but first . . .

WELCOME AND PROCLAIM THE GOSPEL

Say/sing together:

Alleluia, alleluia!
We cannot live on bread alone,
but on every word
that comes from the mouth of God.
Alleluia!

A reading from the Good News given to us by John.
Glory to you, Lord.

After Jesus had fed the five thousand people, the people wanted to make him their king. But Jesus hid from them. So the people set off to find him. When they found him, Jesus said to them
'You're only looking for me because I gave you bread to eat. Don't waste

DISCUSSION

Why, according to Jesus, were the people following him?
How did Jesus feel?
Would you like it if your friends only played with you if you had sweets or money?
What did Jesus promise the people?
When does Jesus give us the bread of life?

A reading from the story of
the Great Escape.

Moses led the people of Israel out of
slavery in Egypt and into the desert
wilderness. After wandering in the
desert for some time, the people
began to grumble and moan:
'We'd rather be back in Egypt! At
least we had enough to eat there!
We're going to starve to death in this
desert!'

God promised Moses the people
would not starve, that he would take
care of them and send them food.
And so it was. Every evening there
were flocks of quail. And every
morning when the dew lifted there
on the surface of the desert was
something fine, white and powdery.
It tasted good, and was called
manna.
So it was that God provided for his
people.

your time working for food that
cannot last, but work instead for the
food of everlasting life.'
The people asked
'How can we do the work God wants
of us?' Jesus replied
'You work for God when you believe
in the one whom he has sent.' The
people said
'Show us a sign, like Moses giving
our forefathers manna in the desert,
then we will believe in you.'

Jesus replied
'It wasn't Moses, but God who fed
them in the desert. God has true
bread for you, too.'
The people asked
'Give us that bread always.'
Jesus said
'I am the bread of life. Whoever
comes to me will never be hungry
again.'
This is the Gospel of the Lord.
Praise to you, Lord Jesus Christ.

ACTIVITIES

> Give out the cut-out shapes.

> Have the children write or draw
  on them a thank you to Jesus for
  giving himself to us in
  communion.

> Collect all the work on to the
  golden plate.

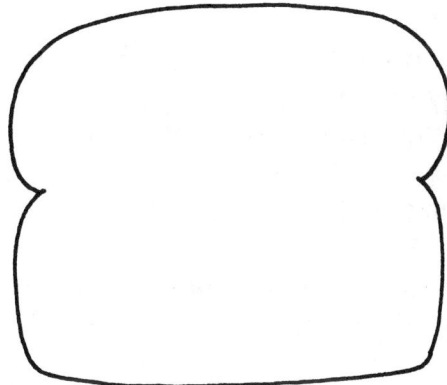

JESUS IS THE LIVING BREAD

VISUAL AIDS

> Pictures of people travelling, sharing meals, sharing picnics.

> Bread or bread rolls.

> The golden plate (see last week)

> Altar bread shape cut-outs.

WELCOME AND PROCLAIM THE GOSPEL

Say/sing together:

**Alleluia, alleluia!
Jesus is the living bread
who has come down from heaven.
Alleluia!**

A reading from the Good News given to us by John.
Praise to you, Lord Jesus Christ.

After Jesus said 'I am the bread that came down from heaven' the people started to grumble and complain. 'What is he talking about! We know he's Joseph's son, so how can he be from heaven!'
Jesus said
'Stop complaining. I am the bread of

DISCUSSION

What does Jesus say about bread in today's story?
- that he is the bread sent from heaven.
When does Jesus offer us this special bread?
How do we prepare for this special food?

ACTIVITIES

> Give out the altar bread shape cut-outs.

> On them have the children write a prayer asking Jesus to help them on their journey next week.

> Collect the 'breads' on to the golden plate.

SHARING

Using the pictures, encourage the children to share journey experiences, and especially ways of eating when travelling: picnics; cafés; buffets; etc.

Life, too, is a journey. Where to?
- heaven.
We need food for the journey.

God gives us the food for the journey, which is Jesus himself. Jesus gives us the strength we need for the long journey home to our Father in heaven.

life which has come down from heaven. Anyone who eats this bread will live forever. The bread I shall give is myself for the life of the world.'

This is the Gospel of the Lord.
Praise to you, Lord Jesus Christ.

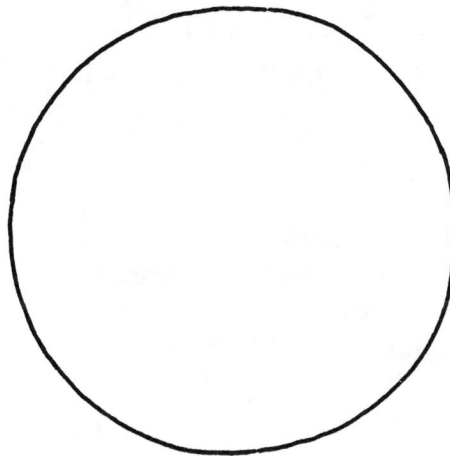

> Recite this psalm, all saying the response, different groups for each verse:

Response: **Taste and see that the Lord is good.**
I will bless the Lord always, sing his praise for ever.
I will boast of his goodness to me.
Good people will rejoice with me.
Response.

Glorify the Lord with me.
Let us together praise his name.
For God answers my prayers and cares for my every need.
Response.

Look to God for all your needs.
No need to be scared.
Taste, and you too will discover how good the Lord is.
Response.

REJOICE! JESUS IS OUR BREAD

VISUAL AIDS

> Contrasting pictures of growth and destruction.

> Pictures of people helping each other.

> Bread or bread rolls.

> Altar bread shape cut-outs.

WELCOME AND PROCLAIM THE GOSPEL

Say/sing together:

**Alleluia, alleluia!
Lord, give us the living bread
from heaven.
Alleluia!**

A reading from the Good News given to us by John.
Praise to you, Lord Jesus Christ.

Jesus says:

'I am the bread of life
which has come down from heaven.

Anyone who eats this bread
will live for ever.

DISCUSSION

What does Jesus say he will give us?
- himself, given for the life of the world.

When does Jesus give himself for the life of the world?
- on the cross.

When does Jesus give himself to be our food?
- in communion.

SHARING

How does bread help us?
- it gives us strength
- it keeps us alive.

It is good to be alive in such a wonderful world.

When we are alive we can work to make the world an even more beautiful and happy place.

Encourage the children to give examples.

Conclude the sharing by saying/ singing a Gloria together in praise and thanks for being alive.

The bread that I shall give
is myself
for the life of the world.'

This is the Gospel of the Lord.
Praise to you, Lord Jesus Christ.

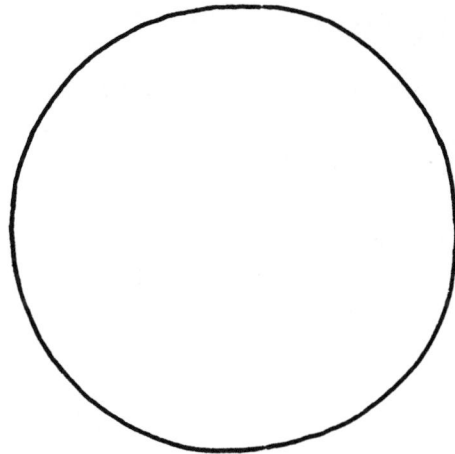

ACTIVITIES

> Give out the altar bread cut-out shapes.

> On them have the children write or draw:
something they will do for Jesus in the coming week;
something that makes them happy.

> Recite this prayer together, the children repeating it line by line:

God our Father,
thank you for giving us Jesus
to be our bread of life.
Help us to love you
above all things
and to reach the joy
you have prepared for us.
Help us to spread your happiness
here on earth.

YOU HAVE THE MESSAGE OF ETERNAL LIFE

VISUAL AIDS

> Pictures relating to communication e.g. letters, telephone, TV, radio, newspapers, etc.

WELCOME AND PROCLAIM THE GOSPEL

Say/sing together:

**Alleluia, alleluia!
Lord, you have the message
of eternal life.
Alleluia!**

A reading from the Good News given to us by John.
Glory to you, Lord.

When Jesus said
'I am the living bread;
anyone who eats my flesh
and drinks my blood
will have eternal life'
many of the people listening were very upset.

DISCUSSION

What was sad in today's story?
- that some of Jesus' friends left him.

Why did they turn away from him?

How do you think Jesus felt?

Did he change his message?
- no!

Why not?
Who did believe?

Encourage the children to listen carefully to the eucharistic prayer when they return to the church, especially the words of consecration:
'Take this, all of you, and eat it:
this is my body
which will be given up for you.'

SHARING

How did Jesus spread the Good News?

If Jesus were in the world today, how do you think he might spread the message?

Would he use radio, TV, etc.?

What is his message?
- love.
How is the message of love spread?

Encourage the children to offer examples.

Today's story is a little sad. Listen carefully, and think what you would have done if you were there.

'This is shocking!' they said, 'How can anyone accept this?' Many of the people left Jesus and went away.

Jesus said to his twelve special friends
'Do you want to leave me, too?'
Peter answered,
'Lord, to whom shall we go? You have the message of eternal life. We believe, we know that you are the Holy One of God.'

This is the Gospel of the Lord.
Praise to you, Lord Jesus Christ.

ACTIVITIES

> Give the children blank paper, and:

either, have them write a prayer asking Jesus for help to speak kindly in the coming week;

or, have them draw a picture of a kind action they will do in the week ahead.

LORD, YOUR WORDS ARE LIFE

VISUAL AIDS

> Pictures of people bathing, washing dishes, washing clothes.

> Church shape cut-outs.

WELCOME AND PROCLAIM THE GOSPEL

Say/sing together:

**Alleluia, alleluia!
Your words, Lord, bring us life.
Alleluia!**

A reading from the Good News given to us by Mark.
Glory to you, Lord.

The Pharisees and the Jews in general never eat without first washing their hands. And they have many customs about scrubbing the pots and dishes too.
One day some of the Pharisees and the scribes from Jerusalem noticed that Jesus and his friends began

DISCUSSION

Explain, as necessary, that Pharisees were the ones responsible for the law and customs of the Jews; the Scribes were lawyers, from Jerusalem.

What washing customs are mentioned in the story?
And what did the Scribes and Pharisees notice about Jesus and his friends?

What was Jesus' reply?
What makes people clean in the eyes of God?
Get the children to give examples of things they do because they have to.
And then examples of things they do from the heart.
Do they come to church because they have to?
Or because they want to in their hearts?

SHARING

Invite the children to look at the pictures and encourage them to talk about washing.

What are our reasons for washing things?

Talk about ways of washing, times for washing (e.g. hands before meals).

In Jesus' time too they had customs relating to washing, and when to wash. Jesus will speak about that in today's story.

eating without first washing their hands;
'Why are you breaking our traditions?' they asked Jesus.
Jesus replied
'It is far more important to have clean hearts and clean lives than to have clean hands.'
Then Jesus said to the people,
'It is not what happens on the outside that makes you clean or unclean. It is what you have in your heart that counts. If your heart is full of nastiness, then you will be unclean no matter how much you wash. But if your heart is full of love, you are clean in the eyes of God.'

This is the Gospel of the Lord.
Praise to you, Lord Jesus Christ.

ACTIVITIES

> Give out the church shape cut-outs.

> On them have the children write or draw why they come to church.

> Ask the children to promise that they will be very quiet in church, so as not to disturb the people who are there praying to God in their hearts.

SPEAK, LORD, WE ARE LISTENING

VISUAL AIDS

> Pictures of doctors, nurses, Third World helpers, handicapped children

SHARING

Show the children the pictures and invite them to say what is happening in them.

WELCOME AND PROCLAIM THE GOSPEL

Say/sing together:

**Alleluia, alleluia!
Jesus proclaimed the Good News, cured the people's sickness.
Alleluia!**

A reading from the Good News given to us by Mark.
Glory to you, Lord.

One day, as Jesus was travelling towards the Sea of Galilee, some people brought a man to him who was deaf and who could not speak properly. Jesus took the man aside so that he could be alone with him. Jesus put his fingers in the man's ears, then licked his fingers and put

DISCUSSION

Do the children know anyone who is deaf, or who cannot hear very well?

Do they know anyone who cannot speak very well?

What happened to the man in the story?

Once he was able to speak again, what was it that the man talked about?
- Jesus healing him.

Do the children talk much about the good things that God and Jesus have done for them?

- people are helping each other
- bringing happiness to others.

Today we begin with a psalm about how God helps people.
Have the children say the response after each verse, and invite them to act out the verses as they hear them with simple gestures.

Response:
My soul, give praise to the Lord.

God is faithful forever.
He gives bread to the hungry.

He protects all who call upon him.
He sets prisoners free.

God gives sight to the blind.
He opens the ears of the deaf.

He raises those who feel really
   down.
He protects widows and orphans.

them on the man's tongue. Then, looking up to heaven, he said 'Ephphatha! Be opened'. And immediately the man could hear and speak properly. Jesus told him to tell no one what had happened, but the man was so excited that he told everyone he met. Everyone who heard about it was amazed.

This is the Gospel of the Lord.
Praise to you, Lord Jesus Christ.

ACTIVITIES

> Have the children mime the story. Make sure they express clearly how the man felt when he was cured.

> Explain the meaning of 'Ephphatha', and have the children say this word.
Point out how, to say it properly, you have to use your whole mouth, and open it up wide.

> On blank pieces of paper, ask the children to draw a picture that makes them happy (just as Jesus made the deaf man happy).

> When the picture is finished, have them write a thank you prayer for all the happy events in their lives.

JESUS, YOU ARE THE CHRIST

VISUAL AIDS

> Pictures of Saint Peter, and of the Pope.

> Cross shape cut-outs.

WELCOME AND PROCLAIM THE GOSPEL

Say/sing together:

Alleluia, alleluia!
You are the Christ,
Son of the living God.
Alleluia!

A reading from the Good News given to us by Mark.
Glory to you, Lord.

As they left the village where they had been staying, Jesus said to his friends
'Who do people say that I am?'
They replied
'Some people think you are John the Baptist, come back to life; others say you are a great prophet, like Elijah.'

DISCUSSION

Work through the conversation that Jesus has with Peter.
Notice how sometimes it is God who guides Peter to say the right thing; but sometimes it is the devil who guides him to say the wrong thing.

Why do you think Peter argued with Jesus?

- because he didn't want Jesus to suffer and die.

What was Jesus' answer?
- that both he, and all his followers should take up their cross;
- that by dying, Jesus then rose again to new life, and promises the same for us.

SHARING

Encourage the children to say what they know about the Pope, e.g. what is his name?

Is there anything they know about any of the other Popes?

What do they think the Pope's job is? - basically, it is helping people to know about Jesus, and who he is.

In Jesus' own time lots of people wondered who he was, as we shall hear in today's story.

'And what about you?' said Jesus, 'Who do you say that I am?' Peter spoke up and said 'You are the Christ.' Jesus then began to teach them what it meant for him to be the Christ. That it would mean that he would have to suffer, and that he would die on the cross. Peter got very upset at this, and began to argue with Jesus. Jesus said to him, 'Peter, a moment ago you let God guide you to say I am the Christ. But now it is the devil that is making you argue with me! You must all understand, if you want to be my followers you must each take up your cross. But by dying, you will have new and everlasting life.'

This is the Gospel of the Lord.
Praise to you, Lord Jesus Christ.

ACTIVITIES

> Give out the cross shape cut-outs.

> Have the children write or draw on one side what they believe about Jesus.

> Then on the other side, have them make a badge which says:

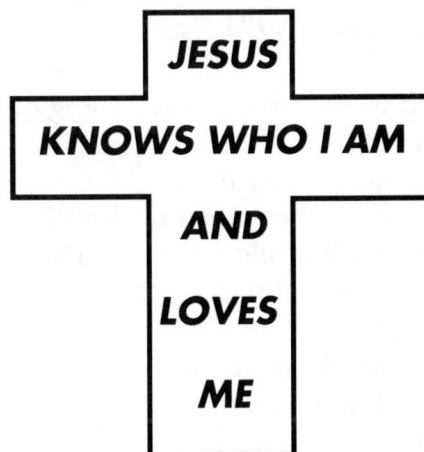

JESUS KNOWS WHO I AM AND LOVES ME

JESUS IS THE GREATEST

VISUAL AIDS

> Pictures of Jesus on the cross, or a crucifix.

> Pictures of important people.

> Round or oval cut-outs (to make badges).

WELCOME AND PROCLAIM THE GOSPEL

Say/sing together:

**Alleluia, alleluia!
I am the light of the world.
Those who follow me
will live in light.
Alleluia!**

A reading from the Good News given to us by Mark.
Glory to you, Lord.

As Jesus and his friends were walking along the road, some of them were arguing with each other. When they reached the house where they were to stay Jesus asked them what they had been arguing about. They did not want to say, because they had been arguing about which

DISCUSSION

What were Jesus' friends doing on the road?
- arguing.
What were they arguing about?
What do the children argue about?
What do they think Jesus would say to them?
What was Jesus' answer?
What does it mean 'to be the servant of all'?

- it means always putting other people first.
What would life be like if everyone did this?
What do you think Jesus meant by what he said about the child?

Jesus is the greatest, yet he was the servant of all. Jesus had time for everyone, even the children.

SHARING

Show the pictures of the important people, and encourage the children to discuss why these people are important.

What have they done?

Who are the most important people in the children's lives?

Why?

In today's Gospel we will hear Jesus tell us who really is the greatest.

---

of them was the greatest.
Jesus sat down, gathered his twelve friends round him and said,
'Whoever wants to be first must be last; the one who wants to be the greatest must be the servant of all.'

Jesus put his arms around a little child and said
'Anyone who welcomes a little child in my name welcomes me; and when you welcome me, you welcome the

one who sent me.'

This is the Gospel of the Lord.
Praise to you, Lord Jesus Christ.

ACTIVITIES

> Together discuss how, in the coming week, we can behave in the way Jesus tells us in the Gospel:
> e.g. no arguing;
> not pushing to be first in line;
> letting others join in games.

> Give out the cut-out shapes.

> Have the children make badges with JESUS IS THE GREATEST written on them. You might arrange these around a picture or statue of Jesus.

ARE YOU FOR ME, OR AGAINST ME?

VISUAL AIDS

> Picture of windmills, yachts, kites.

> Kite shape cut-outs.

WELCOME AND PROCLAIM THE GOSPEL

Say/sing together:

Alleluia, alleluia!
Your word is true, Lord.
Alleluia!

A reading from the Good News given to us by Mark.
Glory to you, Lord.

One day John said to Jesus, 'Master, we have seen a man we don't know casting out devils in your name. But he does not follow you like we do.'
Jesus replied,
'You must not stop him. If he is doing good in my name he will not

DISCUSSION

What did John say to Jesus?

And what did Jesus reply?
Just as you cannot stop the wind from blowing you cannot stop good from being done.

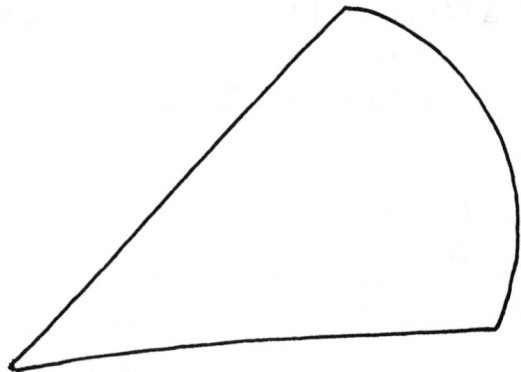

SHARING

What do kites, windmills and yachts all have in common?
- they depend on the wind to make them move
- they show us the power of wind.
Encourage the children to share their experiences of kite flying, yacht sailing, etc.
We cannot see the wind, but we can see what it does.

God's spirit is like the wind. We cannot see the spirit, but we can see what the spirit does.
How? Where?
God's spirit is the spirit of love; the spirit shows in the lives of people who live with love.

In today's Gospel Jesus tells us about God's spirit of love.

harm me. Anyone who is not against us, is for us. Anyone who gives as little as a cup of cold water in my name will be rewarded. But pity help anyone or anything that does get in the way of those who are for me!'

This is the Gospel of the Lord.
Praise to you, Lord Jesus Christ.

ACTIVITIES

> Give out the kite cut-outs.

> Have the children write or draw what it is they would like the spirit to blow them to do in the week ahead.

> Have the children make up a 'Love is . . .' litany, ending with

'Love is being like Jesus, who gave everything for us, even his life.'

27th SUNDAY IN ORDINARY TIME

WE ARE THE FAMILY OF GOD

VISUAL AIDS

> Pictures of families of different nationalities.

SHARING

Invite the children to remember and share memories of happy times they have spent with their families.
What do they like best about their family? What things do they like to

WELCOME AND PROCLAIM THE GOSPEL

Say/sing together:

**Alleluia, alleluia!
If we live in love,
God will live in us.
Alleluia!**

A reading from the Good News given to us by Mark.
Glory to you, Lord.

People were bringing their children to Jesus for him to touch them. Some of Jesus' friends thought the children were being a nuisance, so they began sending them away. When Jesus saw this he said
'Let the children come to me. Do not stop them. It is to these children and

DISCUSSION

What did Jesus' followers think of the children?

So what did they do?

Are we ever like them?

Are there people we think are too much bother, and push them away?

Little brothers and sisters, perhaps?

How did Jesus treat the children?

What do you think he would want us to do?

do with their family?
Today we have a psalm about a
happy family.
All say or sing the response together,
and do the actions during the verses.
Arms raised in prayer
May the Lord bless us all our life.
Mime working actions
Happy are those who love the Lord,
   and follow his ways.
They will find happiness
   in their work. *Response*

*'Wife' in the centre, with a circle of
'children' who dance round her*
Your wife will be the heart
   of your family;
your children will gather round
   in love. *Response*

Children wave and dance around
Happy those who love the Lord.
They and their children's children
   will live in peace. *Response*

those who are like them that the
kingdom belongs.'

Jesus put his arms round the
children, laid his hands on them
and blessed them.

This is the Gospel of the Lord.
Praise to you, Lord Jesus Christ.

ACTIVITIES

> Have the children act out the
  Gospel.

> Give out blank pieces of paper
  and have the children:

  either, draw a picture of happy
  times with their family;

  or, write a prayer for their family.

WE ARE RICH IN JESUS

VISUAL AIDS

> Pictures of rich people.

> Pictures of people helping and sharing.

WELCOME AND PROCLAIM THE GOSPEL

Say/sing together:

Alleluia, alleluia!
Happy are the poor in spirit;
theirs is the kingdom of heaven.
Alleluia!

A reading from the Good News given to us by Mark.
Glory to you, Lord.

Jesus was setting out on a journey when a young man ran up, knelt before him and asked
'Good Master, what must I do to have eternal life?'

Jesus replied
'You know the commandments:

DISCUSSION

What was Jesus doing?
Who came to see him?
What did the young man want?
What advice did Jesus give him?
How did the young man take the advice?
How did the story end?
- the man went away, sad.
If you were the rich young man, what would you have done?

ACTIVITIES

> Let the children take it in turns to act out the story, if possible with modern day equivalents.

> On blank paper have the children write or draw what they will do in the coming week to show how they are following Jesus' advice.

SHARING

Show the pictures to the children and encourage them to talk about what they see in them.
Move the discussion round to asking: what do people value? What do children value most in life? Ask the children for examples of people who use their gifts to help others.

In today's Gospel we will hear about a rich man -
was he happy or sad?

don't kill nor cheat, nor steal nor tell lies; honour your father and mother.'

The young man replied
'Master, I have kept these commandments ever since I was a child.'

Jesus looked at him and loved him, and he said
'There is one thing you have not done. Go, sell everything you own,

give the money to the poor, and you will have treasure in heaven. Then come, follow me.'
When he heard this the man was sad, and went away, for he was very rich.

This is the Gospel of the Lord.
Praise to you, Lord Jesus Christ.

> Join in this prayer:

Let us pray
that we will be satisfied
with the gifts God has given us,
and not want more than we need.
Lord, hear us.
Lord, graciously hear us.

Let us pray
that nothing will hold us back

from following Jesus.
Lord, hear us.
Lord, graciously hear us.

Let us pray
that we will always share
whatever we have with others.
Lord, hear us.
Lord, graciously hear us.

YEAR B
29th SUNDAY IN ORDINARY TIME

JESUS SETS US FREE TO LOVE

VISUAL AIDS

> Pictures of people sitting at table, especially families, or children at a party.

> Party place names.

WELCOME AND PROCLAIM THE GOSPEL

Say/sing together:

**Alleluia, alleluia!
Jesus came to serve,
to give his life for us.
Alleluia!**

A reading from the Good News given to us by Mark.
Glory to you, Lord.

James and John came to Jesus and said
'Master, we want to ask you a favour.'
'What is it?' Jesus asked.
'Allow us to sit with you in glory, one on your right, one on your left.'

DISCUSSION

Who came to ask Jesus a favour?

What was the favour they wanted?

How did Jesus reply?

How did Jesus' other friends feel about all this?

What did Jesus say to them?

What must we do to be a follower of Jesus?

SHARING

Encourage the children to talk about times when they squabble over where to sit, e.g. in the car, at table, in class, etc.

How are places arranged at parties?

What happens when important people are invited to dinner?
At official banquets?

Explain how the guest sits with the host; the custom of sitting at the Captain's table on a ship.
Is it really important where we sit, and who we sit next to?
Are these things worth squabbling about?

Today's Gospel story is about a squabble.

'You don't know what you're asking' said Jesus. 'Can you drink the cup that I must drink? Or be baptised with the baptism I must face?'
'Yes we can', they said.
'Very well, you shall. But the seats on my right and my left aren't mine to give. They have already been set aside for those they belong to.'

Jesus' other friends were annoyed by what John and James had asked for.

Jesus called everyone together and said,
'Don't be like the greedy people of the world. Real greatness comes from serving others. This is what I came to do, to serve others, and to give my life to set them free.'

This is the Gospel of the Lord.
Praise to you, Lord Jesus Christ.

ACTIVITIES

> Have the children act out the Gospel, with the children taking part in the dialogue.

> Have the children write a letter to Jesus, or draw a picture, in which they say/show what they want to be freed from in order to follow him, e.g. to be free of temper; fighting; meanness; squabbling; etc.

> Have the children say what they will do instead, freed from these things.

JESUS, THE LIGHT WITHIN US

VISUAL AIDS

> Pictures of happy people, lights at night, e.g. candles, torches, lanterns, fairy lights, etc.

> A candle or bright light.

> Candle, or lamp, or lantern shape cut-outs.

WELCOME AND PROCLAIM THE GOSPEL

Say/sing together:

Alleluia, alleluia!
Jesus is the light of the world.
Let us follow him.
Alleluia!

A reading from the Good News given to us by Mark.
Glory to you, Lord.

Jesus was on his way out of Jericho with a large crowd of people. A blind man, called Bartimaeus, sat at the roadside, as he always did, begging. When he heard that Jesus was passing, he began shouting 'Jesus, Son of David! Have mercy on me!' The people around him tried to

DISCUSSION

Who was Bartimaeus? And how did he usually spend his days?
What did he want? What did he do?
What did the people think of this?
What did Jesus think?
What did Jesus do for him?
What did Jesus say saved Bartimaeus?
What did Bartimaeus do after he could see again?

Do we see with the light of faith?
- yes, because we are baptised.
What do we see with the light of faith?
- how to follow Jesus.

SHARING

Show the children the pictures and encourage the children to say what makes them happy.
What fills their lives with brightness and light?
How do they bring brightness into the lives of others?
Light the candle or switch on the light.

In today's Gospel we hear about a man who could not see the light.

shush him, but he shouted even louder
'Jesus, Son of David! Have pity on me!'
Jesus stopped and said,
'Bring him here.' To the blind man he said
'Don't worry, it's me, Jesus, calling you.' Bartimaeus jumped up immediately and went to Jesus.
'What do you want from me?' asked Jesus.

'Master, let me see again.'
'Go', said Jesus, 'your faith has saved you.'
Immediately, Bartimaeus could see again, and he followed Jesus along the road.

This is the Gospel of the Lord.
Praise to you, Lord Jesus Christ.

ACTIVITIES

> Have the children act out the Gospel story.

> Give out the cut-out shapes.

> Have the children write or draw on them how they will let the light of faith shine in their lives in the coming week.

BIND US TOGETHER IN LOVE

VISUAL AIDS

> Pictures of families of different nationalities.

> A model castle or toy fort.

> Toy building blocks (e.g. Lego).

> Castle shape cut-outs.

WELCOME AND PROCLAIM THE GOSPEL

Say/sing together:

Alleluia, alleluia!
The Lord is our strength
and our help.
Alleluia!

A reading from the Good News given to us by Mark.
Glory to you, Lord.

One of the Scribes came to Jesus and asked,
'Which is the first of the commandments?'
Jesus replied,
'This is the first: to love the Lord your God with all your heart and with all your strength. The second is

DISCUSSION

Who came to Jesus?
What did he ask?
What was Jesus' reply?

How do we love God with all our heart?
Recall the expression 'to set your heart on . . .'.
Encourage the children to give

examples of things they have set their hearts on.
How could they set their hearts on God?

And how are we to love ourselves?
- by not hurting ourselves.

And how are we to love others?

SHARING

Show the family pictures and encourage the children to talk about their families, to share memories of the happy times they have had together, and of sad times.

What helps a family to be happy?

What helps a family when times are sad?

- their love for each other makes the family strong.

A loving person is a strong person. God's love is the strongest love of all.

Today Jesus shares an important message with us: he tells us how our love can be strong.

this: to love everybody as you love yourself.'
The Scribe said
'Well spoken, Master.'
Jesus said to him
'You yourself are not far from the kingdom of heaven.'
Because Jesus had answered in this way no one else dared question him.

This is the Gospel of the Lord.
Praise to you, Lord Jesus Christ.

ACTIVITIES

> Have the children build 'walls' with the building blocks.
A castle is made up up blocks and bricks bound together. So too we can be as strong as a castle when we are bound together in love.

> Give out the cut-out shapes.

> Have the children write or draw on them a prayer asking God to help them be strong in the week ahead.

TRUST JESUS

VISUAL AIDS

> Pictures of rich and poor people.

> Pictures of people giving and receiving gifts, using their skills to cook, paint, etc.

> Coin shape cut-outs.

> A collecting box.

WELCOME AND PROCLAIM THE GOSPEL

Say/sing:

**Alleluia, alleluia!
Happy are the poor in spirit,
for theirs is the kingdom of heaven.
Alleluia!**

A reading from the Good News given to us by Mark.
Glory to you, Lord.

Jesus was sitting down opposite the collecting box in the Temple, and he watched the people putting their offering in the box. Some of the people who were rich put a great deal of money into the box.
Then along came a poor widow. She put two small coins in the box. They

DISCUSSION

Where was Jesus?
What was he watching?

Which gift did Jesus say was worth most? Why?

Is it only rich people who can give gifts, only grown ups?

What really counts with gifts?
- the love that they stand for.

Encourage the children to offer examples of gifts they can give at home, at church, etc.

SHARING

Encourage the children to talk about gifts they have given and received.

Why do we give gifts?
- to show love, care.

What kinds of gifts are there, apart from presents?
- gifts of time, patience, helping at home, listening at school.

Do we always thank those who give us gifts?
- friends for playing with us; teachers, dinner-ladies, etc?

Do we thank God enough for giving us everything,
but especially for giving us Jesus?

---

were the smallest of all coins, worth less than a penny.
Jesus saw what she put in and said to his friends,
'This poor woman has put more into the box than anyone else. Others gave from what they had to spare; but she put in everything she had, all she had to live on.'

This is the Gospel of the Lord.
Praise to you, Lord Jesus Christ.

ACTIVITIES

> Give out the cut-out shapes.

> On them have the children write or draw about a 'gift' they will offer someone in the week ahead, e.g. a letter, or a visit to a lonely person.

> Collect the 'coins' into the collection box.

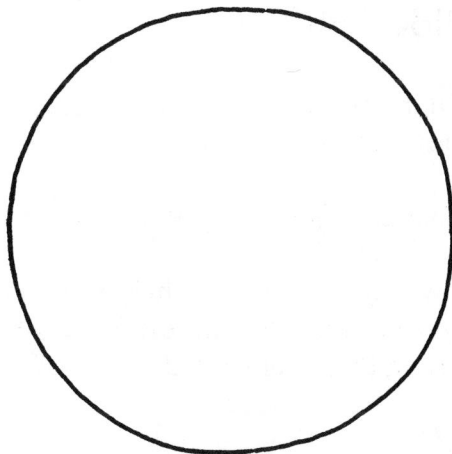

JESUS IS NEAR

VISUAL AIDS

> Pictures of Jesus and children.

> A collection of percussion instruments.

> House shape cut-outs.

WELCOME AND PROCLAIM THE GOSPEL

Say/sing together:

Alleluia, alleluia!
Jesus is with us always.
Alleluia!

A reading from the Good News given to us by Mark.
Glory to you, Lord.

Jesus said to his friends,
'You know by looking at the trees what time of year it is.
So too you will know when terrible things start to happen that the end of the world is near.
The time will come when many things will go wrong;

DISCUSSION

What does Jesus warn his friends about?

What does Jesus promise?

How can the children help to make their homes little kingdoms of God's love in the week ahead? always?

ACTIVITIES

> Give out the percussion instruments.

> Have everyone join in singing/ reciting this psalm, playing instruments or miming to the text:

Response: **The Lord is King forever.**

SHARING

Encourage the children to talk about things that hurt them or make them afraid.

Reassure them that Jesus will always be there to look after them.
Jesus has the power to conquer all badness and to make everything good.

He wants us to be happy with him in his kingdom of love.

In today's Gospel Jesus tells us about his kingdom of love.

many people will be hurt.
But do not be afraid.
I will come and gather all my friends together from every corner of the earth.'

This is the Gospel of the Lord.
Praise to you, Lord Jesus Christ.

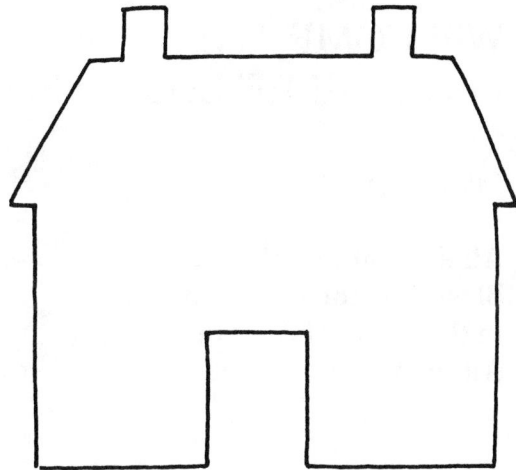

Play the trumpets loud and clear.
Response
Praise God now with tambourine.
Response
Praise him with cymbal and
    booming drums.
Response
Everyone, sing in praise of God.
Response

> Give out the house shapes.

> Have the children draw in the windows, and then write in the windows the names of people they will make happy during the week ahead.

BE ON THE SIDE OF TRUTH

VISUAL AIDS

> Pictures of kings, queens.

> Pictures of people caring for others.

> Picture of Jesus in triumph on the cross.

> Crown shape cut-outs.

WELCOME AND PROCLAIM THE GOSPEL

Say/sing together:

Alleluia, alleluia!
Blessed is the one who comes
in the name of the Lord.
Alleluia!

A reading from the Good News given to us by John.
Glory to you, Lord.

The Gospel can be read in parts
Narrator: Jesus was brought before Pontius Pilate, the Roman Governor who ruled over Palestine.
Pilate: Are you the King of the Jews?
Jesus: Do you ask this because you want to know, or because others

DISCUSSION

Does Jesus say he is a King?
- yes, but not of this world.

Of what, then, is Jesus King?
- he is the King of truth.

What do those who are on the side of truth do?
- listen to his word.

Are we on the side of truth?

How do we show we are on the side of truth?
- by listening to Jesus.

What do we hear when we listen to Jesus?
- how to live truly.

SHARING

Sometimes we speak of an extra special friend being a 'true' friend. What do the children think this means?
- someone who will stand by you, no matter what.

Was Jesus a true friend?
How did he show it?
- by dying to save his friends.

Give examples of people who have been true to Jesus, e.g. martyrs, etc.

How can we be true to Jesus?
- by doing what he asks us;
- by loving his friends as much as he loves them.

Sometimes we are not true or faithful to Jesus. Give examples, and then together say 'We confess . . .'.

have told you to ask this?
Pilate:　I am not Jewish, so why should I want to know? It is your own people, and their chief priests who have handed you over to me. What have you done?
Jesus:　My kingdom is not of this world. If it were I would not be here before you now, for my men would have fought to rescue me.
Pilate:　So you are a King, then?
Jesus:　It is as you say. I was born

for this. I came into the world to do this, to speak up for the truth. All who are on the side of truth listen to me.

Narrator:　This is the Gospel of the Lord.
Praise to you, Lord Jesus Christ.

ACTIVITIES

> Give out the crown shapes.

> On them have the children write or draw:
either, how they will show they are on the side of truth, and of Jesus' Kingdom of love, in the week ahead;
or, what they have heard Jesus say when they listened.

221

YEAR C
2nd SUNDAY IN ORDINARY TIME

BELIEVE!

VISUAL AIDS

> Collection of things associated with weddings, e.g. invitations, decorations, novelties, pictures of weddings.
> Six empty jars, some red food colouring, and a bucket of water.
> B E L I E V E in large, individual cut-out letters.
> Water drop shape cut-outs.
> Cut-out water jar.

WELCOME AND PROCLAIM THE GOSPEL

Say/sing together:

**Alleluia, alleluia!
Jesus let his glory be seen
so that we may believe in him.
Alleluia!**

A reading from the Good News given to us by John.
Glory to you, Lord.

Jesus, his mother Mary and many of his friends were invited to a wedding in a town called Cana.
But in the middle of the reception, they ran out of wine! When she heard this Mary said to Jesus 'They have no wine.' Jesus answered 'Why tell me?'

DISCUSSION

Encourage the children to retell the story in their own words.

Remind them of the last part, where we are told this sign was to let Jesus' glory be seen, so that we might believe. Those who believe in Jesus give him glory.
Remember the Gloria sung by the angels at Jesus' birth.

For those who believe, the whole world is full of God's glory.
For those who believe, the little drops of water of everyday life are changed, if we do them for Jesus.

Encourage the children to give examples of 'water drops', e.g. smiles, kindness, sharing.

SHARING

Encourage the children to share their experiences of weddings, and wedding receptions.

What would it be like if they ran out of food or drinks at a wedding?

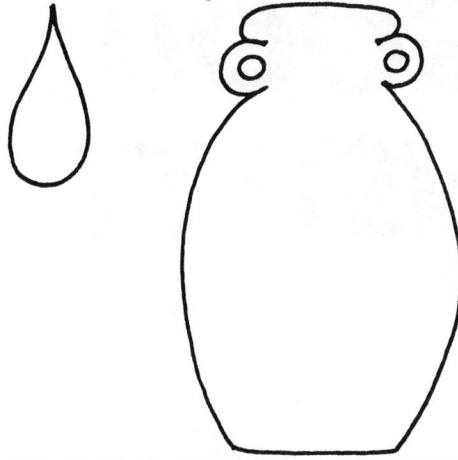

Mary said to the servants 'Do whatever Jesus tells you to do.' Nearby there were six stone water jars, which each held about a hundred litres. Jesus said to the servants 'Fill the jars with water.' They filled them to the brim. 'Now draw some out' said Jesus, 'and take it to the head waiter.' The servants did as Jesus said. The head waiter tasted the water, which had turned into wine. He didn't know where it had come from, so he said to the bridegroom 'This is wonderful wine. Why didn't you serve this wine to your guests first?' This was the first sign that Jesus worked so that his glory might be seen, and that people might believe in him.

This is the Gospel of the Lord. **Praise to you, Lord Jesus Christ.**

ACTIVITIES

> Have the children act out the Gospel. Make sure that the six jars have a little red food colouring in them beforehand, so that when the water is added it will look like wine!

> Give out the cut-out shapes.

> Have the children write or draw on them what they want to change for Jesus in the week ahead.

> Some of the children could decorate the letters of B E L I E V E and fasten them on to the cut-out water jar.

> Collect the water drops and fasten them on to the cut-out water jar.

223

GOOD NEWS!

VISUAL AIDS

> A Bible on a stand or a cushion.

> A scroll, tied with ribbon.

> G O O D N E W S in large, individual cut-out letters.

> Small scrolls, one for each child.

WELCOME AND PROCLAIM THE GOSPEL

Say/sing together:

Alleluia, alleluia!
The Lord has sent me to proclaim
the Good News.
Alleluia!

A reading from the Good News given to us by Luke.
Glory to you, Lord.

Jesus, filled with the power of the Spirit, travelled around the villages of Galilee preaching and teaching the people. Everyone praised him. He came to Nazareth where he had been brought up. On the sabbath day he went with everyone else to the synagogue. There they asked

DISCUSSION

What did Jesus do?
- travelled around, teaching and preaching.
What town did he come to?
- Nazareth.
Why was this town special to Jesus?
- this is where Jesus was brought up.
Where did he go on the sabbath?
- to the synagogue.

What happened?
- he was asked to read.
What did he read?
- an extract from the prophet Isaiah.
What did the reading say?
What did Jesus say?
What would be good news to a blind person? a deaf person? etc.?
What good news have the children had that made them happy?

SHARING

Show the children the Bible. Explain how and why we treat it with reverence and honour.
- because it is a special book
- because it is the book of God's Word
- it is the story of God's love for us.

Encourage the children to share what they know about the Bible, their favourite Bible stories.
Perhaps some of the children have parents, grandparents, big brothers or sisters, who are readers at Sunday Mass. Would they like to be readers when they are older?

Today we hear the story of one day in the synagogue when Jesus was asked to be the reader. In those days they did not have books, but a scroll.

him to read, so he stood up and the assistant handed him the scroll of the prophet Isaiah. Jesus unrolled the scroll, found the place and began to read:
'The spirit of the Lord has been given to me;
he has called me and set me apart.
I have to preach good news to the poor;
to tell prisoners they can go free;
to bring sight to the blind;
to set the downtrodden free;
to tell everyone that the good news of the Kingdom is here.'
Jesus rolled up the scroll and gave it back to the assistant. Everyone was watching him. Then he said
'The words that you have just heard are coming true in me.'

This is the Gospel of the Lord.
Praise to you, Lord Jesus Christ.

ACTIVITIES

> Have the children mime the Gospel story.
> Give out the individual scrolls.
> Have the children write or draw on them:
  either some good news which made them happy;
  or a thank you prayer for good news they have had.

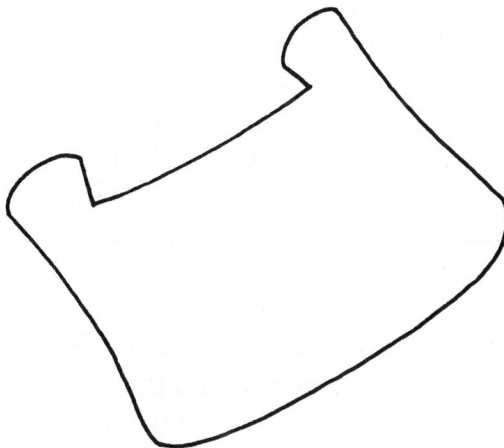

BE
TRUE

VISUAL AIDS

> A Bible on a stand or a cushion.
> A scroll tied with a ribbon.
> The theme BE TRUE on a large heart shape.
> Pictures of a range of different people.
> Heart shape cut-outs.

WELCOME AND PROCLAIM THE GOSPEL

Say/sing together:

**Alleluia, alleluia!
The Lord has sent me
to proclaim the Good News.
Alleluia!**

A reading from the Good News given to us by Luke.
Glory to you, Lord.

After reading from the prophet Isaiah in the synagogue Jesus began to speak:
'The words you have just heard are coming true today in me.' The people were amazed, because he made the scriptures so clear by the way he read and explained them.

DISCUSSION

Recap as much as may be necessary from last week: that Jesus is in his home town; he has just read from the scroll of Isaiah; and said that the prophecy is coming true in him.

Why did the people begin to mutter, and then get angry with Jesus?
- because they didn't like what he said.

What did they not like?
- that someone they knew should be telling them how to behave
- that he told them to stop being selfish, etc.

Do the children think the people wanted to change their lives?
- no. They closed their hearts to Jesus.

SHARING

Show the pictures of the different people;
encourage the children to look at each other and to notice their differences.
Would their parents notice if a different child took their place? Why?
Ask the children to sit in a circle, to hold hands, and to recite line by line:

We are all different.
We look different.
We feel different.
We think differently.
We walk differently.
We talk differently.
But we try to love each and everyone as they are.
We do not pretend to be what we are not.
We try to be true to ourselves.

Many people, though, began to mutter against Jesus, saying
'Who does he think he is? We know he is only the carpenter's son.'
Jesus continued speaking.
'The Kingdom of God is here. You must change your ways, turn from your selfishness.' Then the people got angry and threw him out of the synagogue.
This is the Gospel of the Lord.
Praise to you, Lord Jesus Christ.

ACTIVITIES

> Give out the cut-outs.

> On them have the children write or draw:
some of the people they know;
and a prayer asking that they will never close their hearts to Jesus.

> Have the children act out the Gospel story, if possible with modern day equivalents.

FOLLOW ME

VISUAL AIDS

> Pictures of boats, fishing.

> Fishing nets, fish, seashells.

> Fish shape cut-outs.

WELCOME AND PROCLAIM THE GOSPEL

Say/sing together:

**Alleluia, alleluia!
Follow me, says the Lord,
and I will make you fishers of men.
Alleluia!**

A reading from the Good News given to us by Luke.
Glory to you, Lord.

Jesus was standing one day by the lakeside, where a huge crowd gathered to hear him speak. Jesus saw a couple of boats nearby, so Jesus climbed into one of them, belonging to Simon. Jesus asked Simon to sail a little way out from the shore. From there he spoke to the

DISCUSSION

Have the children retell the story in their own words.

Why does Jesus first get into the boat?
- to speak to the crowds better.
What happens then?
- he tells the fishermen to put their nets out.

What happens?

How do the fishermen react?
- amazed and a bit bewildered.

What does Jesus say to them?
- follow me.

SHARING

Encourage the children to share their experiences of fishing, of sailing, of the seaside.

Do they think being a fisherman is easy? Explain that it is a dangerous way of life, and often unpleasant, especially having to go to sea in winter storms.

Today Jesus will will say something else is like fishing. Listen carefully and see what it is.

crowd on the shore.
When he had finished he told Simon to sail out into the deep water and to throw his nets over for fish. Simon said
'We've been fishing all night and caught nothing. But if you say so, we'll try again.'
Simon and the other fishermen threw the nets into the lake, and caught so many fish that the nets began to tear and the weight nearly made the boats sink.
Simon, and the other fishermen, James and John, were amazed.
Simon knelt down at Jesus' knees and said
'Leave me, Lord. I am a sinful man.'
Jesus said
'Don't be afraid, from now on you will be fishers of men.'

This is the Gospel of the Lord.
Praise to you, Lord Jesus Christ.

ACTIVITIES

> Have the children act out the story; have them take the part of the crowd, and the fish, as well as Jesus and the fishermen.

> Give out the cut-out shapes.

> Have the children write or draw on them how they will follow Jesus in the week ahead.

> Collect the fishes into a net.

HAPPINESS BRINGS PEACE

VISUAL AIDS

> Several pictures of happy people, pasted on individual cards with the words HAPPINESS IS . . .

> Blank pieces of card, divided into eight sections

WELCOME AND PROCLAIM THE GOSPEL

Say/sing together:

**Alleluia, alleluia!
Happy are those who hear
the word of God
and keep it.
Alleluia!**

A reading from the Good News given to us by Luke.
Glory to you, Lord.

Jesus climbed up a little hill where he sat down. His friends went with him and a crowd of people followed them. Jesus sat down and began to speak to them:
'Happiness is putting God first.
Happiness is being kind and gentle.
Happiness is being truthful and

DISCUSSION

Who can remember what ways of being happy that Jesus gave us?

Does Jesus give any other ways of being happy?

Has anyone ever tried any of the ways of Jesus?

What happened?

SHARING

Give out the picture cards, and have the children complete them with words which describe the activity in the picture. It may help to discuss what the scenes show as they work.

Lead the children to see that all the happy scenes are also scenes of peace: no one is fighting or quarrelling.

This is why they are happy.

Have the children share their ideas on how they might change unhappiness into happiness.

Today Jesus tells us how we can be happy.

honest.
Happiness is sharing what you have.
Happiness is being peaceful.
Happiness is being ready to suffer for God.
Happiness is rejoicing that your reward is very great in heaven.'

This is the Gospel of the Lord.
Praise to you, Lord Jesus Christ.

ACTIVITIES

> Next week is going to be experiment week: we are going to experiment with the ways that Jesus gave us for being happy. Try a different way each day.

> Give out the blank cards, and explain to the children that each day when they have experimented they tick the card.

1	5
2	6
3	7
4	8

SHARE WHAT YOU HAVE

VISUAL AIDS

> An attractive container overflowing with wrapped gifts, i.e. small novelties, one for each child.

> A card for each child with the words I WILL SHARE . . .

WELCOME AND PROCLAIM THE GOSPEL

Say/sing together:

Alleluia, alleluia!
Love one another
as God loves everyone.
Alleluia!

A reading from the Good News given to us by Luke.
Glory to you, Lord.

Jesus says to his friends,
'You must be like your Father in heaven,
full of pity and mercy.
Never judge anyone.
Never condemn anyone.
Always forgive everyone.

DISCUSSION

Jesus says we must be like someone: who is it we should be like?

In what ways can we be like our Father in heaven?
- in being generous,
- in showing love,
- in being forgiving, etc.

What will God do when we give what we have?
- God will repay us;
- no matter how generous we are to others, God will be even more generous to us.

SHARING

God gives us all many gifts.
God shares everything he has with us.

Encourage the children to give examples.

We all love to receive gifts, and today there are some gifts for sharing -

but first Jesus tells us how we can be more like God our Father who is so generous to us all.

Whatever you give one another,
God will always give you more.
God's gifts will be more
than you can ever imagine;
his gifts will be overflowing.'

This is the Gospel of the Lord.
Praise to you, Lord Jesus Christ.

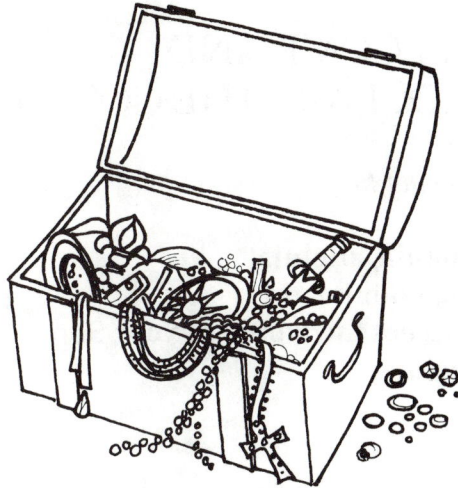

ACTIVITIES

> Have the children mime ways of being like God, e.g. sharing gifts.

> Share out the gifts from the container amongst the children.

> Give out the cards, and have the children complete them, writing a gift they can share with another:

e.g.
'I will share a smile';
'. . . a kind word';
'. . . helping hand';
'. . . time'.

LOOK AND SEE

VISUAL AIDS

> Pictures of scenery, people, animals, trees.

> A collection of differently coloured paper.

> A log of wood, some sawdust.

> Tree shape cut-outs.

WELCOME AND PROCLAIM THE GOSPEL

Say/sing together:

**Alleluia, alleluia!
Open our hearts
to accept the words of your Son.
Alleluia!**

A reading from the Good News given to us by Luke.
Glory to you, Lord.

Jesus said to his friends,
'Can one blind person show another blind person the way?
Won't they end up both falling over something?
And why is it that people are too quick to pick out faults in those around them, but can't see their own

DISCUSSION

Go over the three sets of questions Jesus asks in the Gospel, and get the children to answer them:
- blind leading the blind;
- splinter in the eye;
- good and bad fruit.

Have the children give examples of what would be 'good fruit' for them,

e.g. seeing where help is needed and giving it; seeing someone who is lonely and being a friend to them.

SHARING

Show the pictures to the children
and ask them what they can see.
Show the paper, and ask what is
their favourite colour.
What is their favourite sight?
When did seeing someone, seeing
something make them really happy?
Talk about the many wonderful
things in the world there are to see
and enjoy.

faults?
It's like saying to someone "You've
got a speck of dust in your eye"
while you've got a plank in your
own eye!
Do you expect to pick figs from
thorns? Or grapes from brambles?
People are just the same: by what
they show you can know what is in
their heart.
If their heart is bad it will show in
the way they behave badly.

If their heart is full of goodness, it
will show in the way they behave
well.'

This is the Gospel of the Lord.
Praise to you, Lord Jesus Christ.

ACTIVITIES

> Have the children act out 'good'
  and 'bad' trees.

> Give out the cut-outs.

> On them have the children write
  or draw how they will use their
  eyes, their gift of sight lovingly to
  produce good fruit in the week
  ahead.

FRIENDSHIP IS BRINGING JESUS TO EACH OTHER

VISUAL AIDS

> Pictures, cards or posters depicting friends, friendship.

WELCOME AND PROCLAIM THE GOSPEL

Say/sing together:

Alleluia, alleluia!
God loved the world so much
he gave his only Son.
Alleluia!

A reading from the Good News given to us by Luke.
Glory to you, Lord.

Jesus came to Capernaum, a town which had a camp of Roman soldiers. The centurion, the head soldier, had a servant who was very sick, and near to death. The centurion heard about Jesus, so he sent for the Jewish leaders to ask them to bring Jesus to heal his

DISCUSSION

Explain, as necessary, that a centurion had charge of a hundred soldiers.
Did the Jewish people usually like the Roman soldiers?
- no. They thought of them as enemies.
Did they like this soldier?
- yes.

Why?
- because he had helped the town; built the synagogue.
How did Jesus help the centurion?
What message did the centurion send?
What was Jesus' response?

SHARING

Encourage the children to talk about
their friends. Who are their friends?
Who is their best friend?
What does it mean to be a friend?
What do they enjoy with friends?

Our best friend is Jesus.
Today's Gospel is the story of a man
who came to be a friend of Jesus
because he was a friend to others.

servant. The leaders pleaded with
Jesus:
'This centurion deserves a
favour, he has been very good to the
town. Why, he even built the
synagogue.'
So Jesus went with them towards the
centurion's house. But before they
reached it, the centurion sent word
to Jesus to say
'Sir, don't put yourself to the trouble
of coming to the house. Just as I can
order my soldiers, so you can order
the illness to leave my servant. I am
not worthy to have you under my
roof.' When Jesus heard this, he said
to everyone around him,
'This man, a pagan, has shown more
faith than any of God's chosen
people.' When the servants returned
to the centurion's home, they found
the servant healed.
This is the Gospel of the Lord.
Praise to you, Lord Jesus Christ.

ACTIVITIES

> Have the children act out the
  Gospel.

> Ask the children to sit quietly and
  think about their friends.

> Give out blank paper and ask the
  children:
  either, to draw a picture of their
  best friend;

or, write how they can be a better
friend.

THANK YOU FOR THE GIFT OF NEW LIFE

VISUAL AIDS

> A selection of things connected with celebration, e.g. greetings cards, party hats, etc.

> Blank cards.

WELCOME AND PROCLAIM THE GOSPEL

Say/sing together:

Alleluia, alleluia!
God has visited his people.
Alleluia!

A reading from the Good News given to us by Luke.
Glory to you, Lord.

Just as Jesus and his friends were coming into a town called Nain, they met a funeral carrying out a dead man to be buried. He was the only son of his mother, and she was a widow. When Jesus saw her he felt sorry for her.
'Don't cry' he said. Then Jesus went

DISCUSSION

Have the children retell the Gospel story in their own words.
What gift did Jesus give to the mother?
What gift did Jesus give the son?
- new life.

Jesus gave us new life by dying on the cross and by rising again.

When Jesus gave the young man new life, what did the people do?
- praised God.

On Sunday we come to Mass to praise God for the new life we have received.

SHARING

Show the visual aids to the children then encourage them to talk about their favourite celebrations.
Why do we celebrate?
- to share happiness with other people.

Each Sunday God invites us to his celebration, at his table in his house.

This is called 'eucharist', which means thanksgiving.

Can the children think of any other thanksgiving celebrations?
For what do we give thanks at the eucharist?

up to the stretcher, and put his hand on it. The bearers stood still. Jesus said
'Young man, I tell you, get up!'
The dead man sat up and began to talk.
Jesus gave him to his mother.
Everyone was amazed and began to praise God.

This is the Gospel of the Lord.
Praise to you, Lord Jesus Christ.

ACTIVITIES

> Have the children act out the story.

> Have the children make a thank you card for God, thanking him for the gift of new life given to us in baptism.

> The children can write or draw what they most want to thank God for.

GO IN PEACE

VISUAL AIDS

> Pictures of people sharing meals.

> Attractive perfume or oil containers.

> Perfume.

> Fancy bottle or jar shape cut-outs.

WELCOME AND PROCLAIM THE GOSPEL

Say/sing together:

Alleluia, alleluia!
God loved us so much he sent his
**   only Son**
to take our sins away.
Alleluia!

A reading from the Good News given to us by Luke.
Glory to you, Lord.

One day a Pharisee named Simon invited Jesus to his house for a meal. While they were eating a woman came into the house. She had a bad name in the town. She had heard Jesus was dining with Simon and had come to find him, bringing a jar of very expensive perfume. She knelt

DISCUSSION

Have the children retell the story of Jesus coming to dinner with Simon.

Why did she pour the perfume on Jesus' feet?
- out of love.

Point out how the smell of perfume spreads everywhere.

What gift did Jesus give her?
- forgiveness and peace.

Like the perfume, Jesus' peace and forgiveness can spread everywhere, to everyone.

SHARING

Invite the children to guess the connection between perfume and meals
- e.g. that people wear perfume (or aftershave) when they go out for a special meal.
Let the children smell the perfume, and invite them to discuss the smells.
Talk about the use of oils for anointing. Oils are used to look after your body, your skin.
Some oils are used to honour people in special circumstances
e.g. kings and queens are anointed at their coronation
e.g. we are anointed in baptism and confirmation.
This anointing is a sign of having become God's children. God's anointing is a sign of his great love for us.

at Jesus' feet. She was crying, and her tears fell on Jesus' feet, so she wiped them with her hair. She kissed Jesus' feet and poured the perfume over them. Simon thought to himself 'If Jesus really were a great prophet, he'd know what kind of woman this is.' Jesus looked at Simon and said 'Imagine two people owe a man money; one owes a few pence, the other many pounds. They are both pardoned. Which do you think will love him more?' Simon answered 'The one who owed more.'
'Exactly', said Jesus. 'You didn't kiss me, nor offer me water to wash my feet. This woman has done it with her tears. She has shown great love because her many sins have been forgiven.' Turning to the woman Jesus said 'Go in peace, your faith has saved you.'
This is the Gospel of the Lord.
Praise to you, Lord Jesus Christ.

ACTIVITIES

> Have the children act out the Gospel.

> Give out the cut-out shapes.

> Have the children write or draw on them ways in which they can pour out love and forgiveness in the week ahead.

> Have the children sit quietly, and think about something for which they are sorry. Anoint each child with perfume, saying 'Jesus forgives you. Go in peace.'

FOLLOW ME

VISUAL AIDS

> A collection of flags, emblems, badges, etc., of clubs, teams, countries.

> A cross.

> Cross shape cut-outs.

WELCOME AND PROCLAIM THE GOSPEL

Say/sing together:

Alleluia, alleluia!
Anyone who follows me
will have the light of life.
Alleluia!

A reading from the Good News given to us by Luke.
Glory to you, Lord.

One day, after he had been praying, Jesus said to his friends,
'If you want to follow me,
you will not find it easy.

If you want to follow me,
you will have to give up your own way.

DISCUSSION

Jesus is our leader:
what does he say to us?

How does he speak to us?

What kind of people does he want us to be?
Jesus is our leader.
His sign is the cross.

Why is his sign the cross?
What does the cross stand for?

In what ways do we find it hard to follow Jesus?
What are our crosses?
What did Jesus do for us?

SHARING

Once upon a time there were two great leaders: one was very bad and one was good and kind. From time to time these leaders called their followers to speak to them.
What kind of place do you think the bad leader would have ready for his followers?
What do you think he would say to them?

What tone of voice? What might he ask them to do?
And the good leader: what kind of place would he choose? What would he say? What tone of voice?
What would he want his followers to do?

Listen now to Jesus as he speaks to us.

Every day you will have to take up your cross and follow me.

I am ready to suffer and die for you.

Anyone who follows me
must be ready to do the same.'

This is the Gospel of the Lord.
Praise to you, Lord Jesus Christ.

ACTIVITIES

> Give out the cross shapes.

> On them have the children write or draw:
  either, the things they find hard;
  or, the help they need to follow Jesus;
  or, a way in which they will try to follow Jesus.

FOLLOW ME

VISUAL AIDS

> A selection of pictures about travelling.

> Pictures of people arriving and departing.

> A bird's nest (or a picture of one).

> Paper and sticks to make flags.

WELCOME AND PROCLAIM THE GOSPEL

Say/sing together:

Alleluia, alleluia!
Lord, show us the path of life.
Alleluia!

A reading from the Good News given to us by Luke.
Glory to you, Lord.

Jesus set out on the road towards Jerusalem. Some friends went ahead to prepare the way for them. One village didn't want to receive Jesus, which made the messengers very annoyed. But Jesus simply went to another village instead.
As they travelled along they met a

DISCUSSION

Who did Jesus meet on the road?

What did the first man say?
How did Jesus reply?

What did the second man say?
How did Jesus reply?

What did the third man say?
How did Jesus reply?

Where do we meet Jesus today?

What does Jesus call us to do for him?

Have the children sit quietly to think of ways in which Jesus calls them and how they can respond.

SHARING

Show the children the pictures of travel, and invite them to talk about journeys they have made to visit people.
Who are the people they like to visit? Why?
What kind of people is it not nice to visit?
- people who are not welcoming.

Today's story is about Jesus on a journey, and a bird's nest.

man who said to Jesus
'I'll follow you wherever you go.'
Jesus said to him
'Foxes have their lairs and birds have their nests, but I have nowhere to lay my head.'
Another man that Jesus invited to follow him said
'First let me bury my father, who has just died.' Jesus told him that the spreading of the kingdom was more important than any one person.

A third person who wanted to follow Jesus asked if he could say farewell to his family first. Jesus replied 'You must make up your mind what you want to do, and then do that. Anyone who looks back after setting out with me is not fit for the Kingdom of heaven.'

This is the Gospel of the Lord.
Praise to you, Lord Jesus Christ.

ACTIVITIES

> Have the childen act out the Gospel.

> People who follow a leader sometimes wave a flag to show who they follow. Have the children make a flag which shows that they are for Jesus.

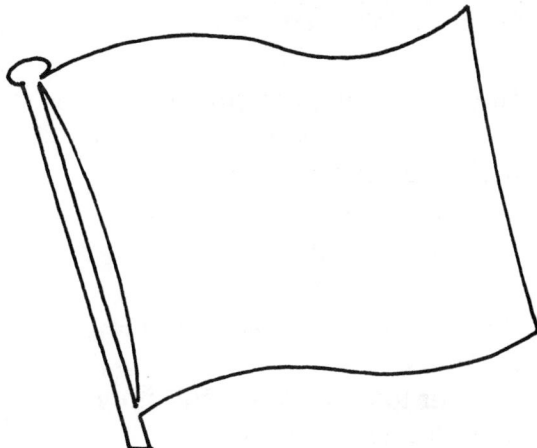

YOUR NAME IS WRITTEN IN HEAVEN

VISUAL AIDS

> Pictures of or books about famous people who have helped human-kind, e.g. Florence Nightingale, Columbus, etc.

> A card for each child on which is written
MY NAME . . . IS WRITTEN IN HEAVEN.

WELCOME AND PROCLAIM THE GOSPEL

Say/sing together:

Alleluia, alleluia!
Rejoice, because
your names are written in heaven.
Alleluia!

A reading from the Good News given to us by Luke.
Glory to you, Lord.

One day Jesus chose seventy-two people to help him with his work of spreading the Good News. He sent them out before him to all the towns and villages he was planning to visit.

Wonderful things happened for these seventy-two as they went

DISCUSSION

How many helpers did Jesus choose?
Where did he send them, and why?
What happened to them?

How did the helpers return?

What power did Jesus promise them?
- power to defeat harmful things.

What did Jesus say is more important than this?
- it is better to have your name written in heaven than to be powerful.

When are our names written in heaven?
- at baptism.

SHARING

People are sometimes honoured for the work they do, the service they offer.
Have the children give examples of these people.
And do they know how such people are honoured?
With medals, knighthood, freedom of cities, etc.

It is wonderful to use your life to benefit others.

Listen, as Jesus tells us about something which is even more important than doing good works.

about in Jesus' name, healing the sick and proclaiming the Good News.

They came back to Jesus, rejoicing in their success. Jesus rejoiced with them and said
'I have given you my power. Nothing will hurt you, not even serpents and scorpions. But do not rejoice because you have this power. Rejoice instead that your names are written in heaven.'

This is the Gospel of the Lord.
Praise to you, Lord Jesus Christ.

ACTIVITIES

> Have the children divide up into pairs.
> With their partner they say what wonderful things have happened to them.
> Then come back and share this with the whole group.

> Have the children mime the story.

> Give out the cards.

> Have the children fill in their names, and then decorate the card.

MY NEIGHBOUR IS . . .

VISUAL AIDS

> Pictures of roads, travellers, people in need, of people helping the elderly, starving, injured, etc.

> Heart shape cut-outs.

WELCOME AND PROCLAIM THE GOSPEL

Say/sing together:

Alleluia, alleluia!
Those who belong to me
listen to my voice.
I know them and they love me.
Alleluia!

A reading from the Good News given to us by Luke.
Glory to you, Lord.

One day a clever man tried to trick Jesus with this question,
'Who is my neighbour?'
Jesus replied with this story:
'A man was once on his way from Jerusalem to Jericho, when he was attacked by bandits. They took all he had, beat him up, and left him for

DISCUSSION

Have the children retell the story. In particular get them to imagine how the man attacked by bandits would have felt, lying injured while people walked past without helping him.

Do they ever feel like that?
e.g. if no one will play with them at school?

or if others gang up on them, and call them names?

Just as the Samaritan opened his purse to help the wounded man, so Jesus asks us to open our hearts to help others in whatever way we can. Encourage the children to give examples.

SHARING

Show the children the pictures and ask what they show.
- that many people need help
- that different people need different kinds of help
- the many ways in which different people can help.

Why do some people need help?

How are they hurt?

To thank God for all the loving and helping people let us say/sing a Gloria.

dead. Later a priest came along, but when he saw the man he crossed to the other side of the road and passed him by. Then along came one of the Temple assistants, and he too passed by on the other side. Then a foreigner came by, a Samaritan. He felt sorry for the injured man, so he went over to him, cleaned up his cuts and bandaged them. He then lifted the man on to his donkey and took him to an inn, where he carried on looking after him. Next day the Samaritan had to continue on his journey, but left the innkeeper enough money to take care of the man.

Now' said Jesus, 'who was the neighbour to the man who fell into the hands of the bandits?'

This is the Gospel of the Lord.
Praise to you, Lord Jesus Christ.

ACTIVITIES

> Have the children act out the Gospel story.

> Give out the heart shapes.

> On them have the children write about or draw:
either, how they can give love in the week ahead;

or, someone they will make a special effort to help.

ONLY ONE THING IS IMPORTANT

VISUAL AIDS

> Cooking utensils.
> A brush, duster, polish.
> Pictures of people working, people listening.
> A clock.
> Cards with clock faces drawn on them, but no hands.

WELCOME AND PROCLAIM THE GOSPEL

Say/sing together:

**Alleluia, alleluia!
Happy are those
with a generous heart.
Alleluia!**

A reading from the Good News given to us by Luke.
Glory to you, Lord.

Jesus came to a village and went to visit his friends Martha and Mary. Martha welcomed him, and brought him into the house. Martha's sister Mary sat down and listened to Jesus. Meanwhile Martha was busy getting things ready, and serving. She said to Jesus,

DISCUSSION

Who was Jesus going to visit?
- Martha and Mary.

What was Martha doing?
- getting the meal ready.

What was Mary doing?
- listening to Jesus.

What happened then?
- Martha grumbled because Mary wasn't helping.

What was Jesus' answer?
- do what you have chosen to do.

It is important that each one of us should do whatever we can for Jesus.

SHARING

Show the pictures and the household objects.
What do they mean to the children?
- they are all about being busy
- except the listening picture.
The clock is about time.
How do we use our time?
How do we fill it?
Do we have time for others?
little brothers and sisters?
older people?
time to clear and help?
time to pray?
time for Jesus?

Today Jesus talks to his friends about being busy, about the right way to spend their time.

'Lord, don't you care that my sister is leaving me to do all the work by myself? Tell her to help me.' Jesus answered
'Martha, Martha! You worry too much. Mary chose the right thing for her. You should do what you have chosen to do - leave others to do what they have chosen.'

This is the Gospel of the Lord.
Praise to you, Lord Jesus Christ.

ACTIVITIES

> Have the children act out the story, but adding modern day examples, e.g.
- why should I clear up and not you?
- why should I go to bed early?
- why should I go to church?

> Give out the clock faces, and have the children fill in how they spend their Sunday time. How much time is given to Jesus?

LORD, TEACH US TO PRAY

VISUAL AIDS

> Pictures of beautiful people, scenery, animals, birds.

> Flowers, shells, feathers.

WELCOME AND PROCLAIM THE GOSPEL

Say/sing together:

Alleluia, alleluia!
It is the spirit you have received
that makes you pray 'Father'.
Alleluia!

A reading from the Good News given to us by Luke.
Glory to you, Lord.

One day, when Jesus had finished praying, his friends asked him 'Lord, teach us to pray.' This is what Jesus taught them:
'Say this when you pray.
Our Father, who art in heaven, hallowed be thy name.

DISCUSSION

How does today's Gospel begin?
- that Jesus himself had been praying.

What happened next?
- Jesus' friends asked him to teach them to pray.

What did Jesus say?

SHARING

Show the children the pictures and other items.
Then encourage them to share their thoughts on what they see.
What do they think of the world, and all the wonderful animals, etc. that fill it?

Our world is a very beautiful place.

It is God's gift to us.

Let us pray that beauty of the world we see around us will open our eyes to the wonder of God and his love for us.
Sing a song in praise of God's creation, e.g. 'All things bright and beautiful'.

Thy kingdom come.
Thy will be done on earth as it is in heaven.
Give us this day our daily bread.
Forgive us our trespasses as we forgive those who trespass against us.
And lead us not into temptation but deliver us from evil.'

This is the Gospel of the Lord.
Praise to you, Lord Jesus Christ.

ACTIVITIES

> Sing an 'Our Father', with actions.

> Give out blank paper, and ask the children to draw a picture of someone/something that makes them feel like praying.

> Say this prayer, the children repeating it phrase by phrase:

**Father in heaven,
we thank you for all your goodness
  to us.
Fill our hearts with your love.
Help us always to share ourselves
  and what we have
with each other.**

BE FILLED WITH GOD'S LOVE

VISUAL AIDS

> A selection of 'treasures' e.g. jewellery, watches, coins.

> Treasure box shape cut-outs.

WELCOME AND PROCLAIM THE GOSPEL

Say/sing together:

Alleluia, alleluia!
Happy are the poor in spirit;
theirs is the kingdom of heaven.
Alleluia!

A reading from the Good News given to us by Luke.
Glory to you, Lord.

Jesus told the people this story: 'Once there was a very rich man, who had a lot of land and when the crops grew, he had such a huge harvest that he didn't have room to store all the grain in his barns. So he had them pulled down, so that bigger ones could be built. He built

DISCUSSION

Let the children retell the story of the rich man.
What is the message in Jesus' story?
In what ways are people rich in the eyes of God?
- when they are sharing, helpful, kind
- when they are generous with their time, with their gifts.

SHARING

Invite the children to think what is the most precious thing they have. Encourage them to share what they think it is.
How do they treat it?
Are they willing to share it?

Today's Gospel is a story about a very rich man. What did he treasure? Listen carefully and find out.

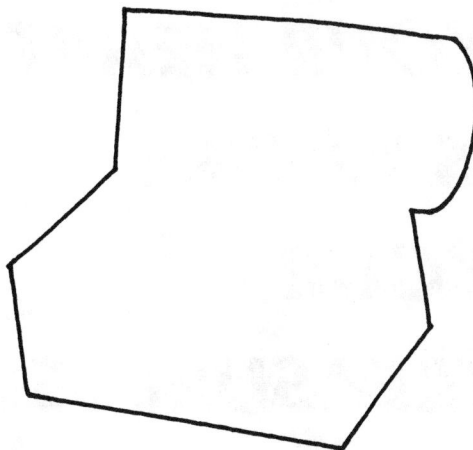

enormous barns in which to store his wealth. When they were ready he felt very pleased, and thought "I've enough to last me for ages. I can now take things easy. I can eat, drink, and not worry about work." But God said to him "Fool! Tonight you are to die, so what good will all this wealth be to you? Everything you have hoarded will be given to someone else." It is better to be rich in the sight of God than to have barns full of wealth.'

This is the Gospel of the Lord.
Praise to you, Lord Jesus Christ.

ACTIVITIES

> Have the children act out the story. Most of the children can be the workers, some to gather in the harvest, the others to knock down the small barns and build bigger ones.

> Give out the 'magic' treasure box shapes.

> Explain that the box is 'magic' because it can only be filled by giving something away; the more we give this thing away the fuller the box becomes.

> Have the children write or draw on the shapes what it is they will give away.

YOUR HEART IS WHERE YOUR TREASURE IS

VISUAL AIDS

> Pictures of rich people and other people sharing.

> Purses, money boxes, money bags, or pictures of them.

> Money bag shape cut-outs.

WELCOME AND PROCLAIM THE GOSPEL

Say/sing together:

Alleluia, alleluia!
Happy are the poor in spirit;
theirs is the kingdom of heaven.
Alleluia!

A reading from the Good News given to us by Luke.
Glory to you, Lord.

Jesus said to his friends,
'Anyone who follows me
need not be afraid,
because God will give you a share
in the Kingdom.

Don't be afraid to sell what you have,
and to share the money you get for it.

DISCUSSION

Why does Jesus say there is no need to be afraid?
- because God will give us a share in the kingdom.

What does Jesus say we should be ready to do?
- to sell, to share.

What treasures should we have, says Jesus?
- treasures in heaven.

What treasures have the children got that they can share?

SHARING

Show the pictures to the children.
What do they all have in common?
- they are all connected with money.
Why do we save money?
Encourage the children to give
examples, e.g. for holidays, to buy
presents for others.
People save until they have enough
money for what they want.

Meantime, many people are afraid
that their money or their treasure
might be stolen.

Listen to what Jesus has to say about
treasure in today's Gospel.

God will reward you with purses
that will never wear out,
or go rusty,
or get eaten by moths.
God will give you treasure in heaven
which no one can steal or destroy.
Your heart is where your treasure is,
so make sure your treasure is in
heaven.'

This is the Gospel of the Lord.
Praise to you, Lord Jesus Christ.

ACTIVITIES

> Give out the cut-out shapes.

> On them have the children write
   or draw:
   either, how they can fill them with
   everlasting treasure;
   or, what they think counts as
   treasure in heaven.

I HAVE COME TO BRING FIRE

VISUAL AIDS

> Pictures of fire.

> Some fired objects, e.g. pottery, metals.

> Flame shape cut-outs.

WELCOME AND PROCLAIM THE GOSPEL

Say/sing together:

Alleluia, alleluia!
Open our hearts, Lord, and
fill them with the fire of your love.
Alleluia!

A reading from the Good News given to us by Luke.
Glory to you, Lord.

Jesus said to his friends,
'I have come to bring fire to the earth,
and how I wish it were blazing already.
It will burn everything clean.
People must make up their minds whether or not they are going to

DISCUSSION

What does Jesus say he has come to bring?
- fire.
What does he want to do?
- set the earth on fire.
What does this mean?

What can fire do?
- it changes things (wood to charcoal);

- it hardens, strengthens things (clay, etc);
- it can melt things (ice, metals);
- it can cook food;
- it can purify (gold).
So what does Jesus mean?
- he has come to change the world;
- to strengthen;
- to burn out the bad, purify what is good;
- to melt hard hearts so they can love again.

SHARING

Encourage the children to say what they know about fire.
It can harm us, hurt us, if we do not treat it with respect.
Fire is very useful and helpful. Have the children give examples
of ways in which we use fire.

In his song in praise of creation, Saint Francis has a verse about fire:

Praise to you, Lord,
for our brother fire.
He is handsome, joyous and
    strong.
Thanks to him, we are kept warm.
Thanks to him, we have light at
    night.

Encourage the children to add other appropriate phrases, or to make up their own song.

follow me.'

This is the Gospel of the Lord.
Praise to you, Lord Jesus Christ.

Jesus wants to change the whole world, to make it new.
When did Jesus send the fire?
- at Pentecost his Spirit appeared like tongues of fire:
- it changed everyone on whom it rested;
- the friends of Jesus were no longer afraid but full of courage;
- they went out to spread the good news of Jesus' love.

ACTIVITIES

> Have the children act out scenes depicting people changing
    - from bad to good
    - from selfishness to generosity
    - from hate to caring.
> Give out the flame cut-outs.
> On them have the children write or draw how they will help spread the message of Jesus' love.

I AM THE WAY

VISUAL AIDS

> Pictures of people of different nationalities.

> Pictures of gateways, doors, entrances.

> Door or gate shape cut-outs.

WELCOME AND PROCLAIM THE GOSPEL

Say/sing together:

Alleluia, alleluia!
I am the way, says the Lord.
Through me you find the Father.
Alleluia!

A reading from the Good News given to us by Luke.
Glory to you, Lord.

Still on their way to Jerusalem,
Jesus and his friends passed through many villages.
In one village someone asked
'Sir, will many be saved, or only a few?'
Jesus replied
'The door to the kingdom of heaven

DISCUSSION

What does Jesus say about the door to the kingdom?
- it is narrow
- locked up for the night.
What does this mean?
- there is only one way in
- not everyone will get through
- it can be easily missed
- we can only enter one by one.

What is the one way?
- it is through Jesus
- by being like Jesus we find our way through to the Father.

SHARING

Show the children the pictures. Can they guess the link?
- doors, gates are for people to go through
- they lead in or out
- we use them to enter, or to leave.
Encourage the children to give as many examples as possible of entrances or doors:

e.g. sliding, automatic, swing, revolving, trap, secret, etc.

In today's Gospel Jesus tells us about the door into the kingdom of heaven.

is narrow, but you must try to get through. Many will try but not all will succeed. Don't leave it too late to knock at the door, If you come to a house too late, after the master has gone to bed and locked everything up, he won't let you in. Many people will try to get in, but many of them will not make it. Those who are shut out will be very sad indeed.'
This is the Gospel of the Lord.
Praise to you, Lord Jesus Christ.

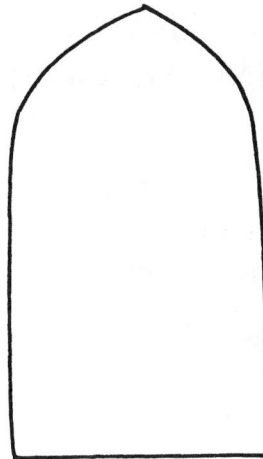

ACTIVITIES

> Have the children act out scenes of people entering through the narrow door, e.g. people showing care, so the door opens for them; making sacrifices for others, etc.

> Give out the door/gate shape cut-outs.

> On them have the children write or draw what it is they will do in the week ahead to make the door open for them.

FRIEND, COME CLOSER TO ME

VISUAL AIDS

> A collection of items connected with parties.

> A selection of invitation cards.

> Bread and cup (chalice) shape cut-outs.

WELCOME AND PROCLAIM THE GOSPEL

Say/sing together:

Alleluia, alleluia!
Learn from me, says the Lord.
Alleluia!

A reading from the Good News given to us by Luke.
Glory to you, Lord.

One day one of the leading Pharisees invited Jesus to his house for a meal. Many others were invited, who watched Jesus to see what he would do. Jesus noticed how as they came in they tried to get the best places at table, the places of honour, so he said,

DISCUSSION

What happened at the meal?
- everyone tried to get the best places.
Which places are best?
- the ones nearest the host.
What advice did Jesus give?
- take a lower place, so that you may be invited higher, rather than have to give your place up to someone more

important and go lower
- always think that others are more important than you.
When do you take the best place?
- in line at school? in the car? for watching TV?
Does Jesus ever invite us to a meal?
- to the eucharist.

SHARING

Using the visual aids, encourage the children to share their memories and experiences of parties.
Who do they invite? And why?
Do they invite only those who will invite them in return?

In today's Gospel story, Jesus has been invited to a meal.

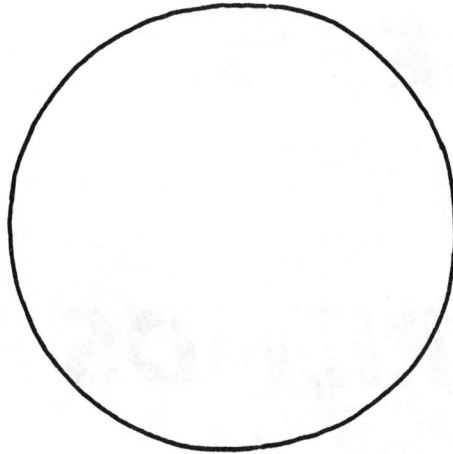

'When you are invited to a wedding feast, don't think you are the most important guest and pick the best place. If you do, and someone more important arrives, you will feel very silly when they have to ask you to take a lower place. No, take a lower place, so you will be told "Come, take a higher place."'
Then Jesus said
'When you give a meal, don't invite only those you know will invite you back in return. No, invite the poor, the lame, the blind. They will not pay you back on earth, but my Father will repay you in heaven.'

This is the Gospel of the Lord.
Praise to you, Lord Jesus Christ.

ACTIVITIES

> Give out the bread/cup cut-outs.

> On them have the children write or draw:
either, the way in which they will give way to others during the week ahead;
or, the way in which they will share with others, as Jesus shares with us in the eucharist.

BE MY FRIENDS

VISUAL AIDS

> Pictures of climbers, builders, soldiers.

> Cross shape cut-outs.

WELCOME AND PROCLAIM THE GOSPEL

Say/sing together:

**Alleluia, alleluia!
Lord, teach us to do
what you want us to do.
Alleluia!**

A reading from the Good News given to us by Luke.
Glory to you, Lord.

Jesus turned to the great crowd that was following him and said 'Following me is not easy. You must know what it will involve.

Suppose you want to build a big tower. You must first sit down and

DISCUSSION

Jesus gives two examples of people working hard to make preparations. What were they?
- building a tower
- going to war.

Why did Jesus tell these stories?
- so that those who want to follow him know what is expected of them.

Jesus says it will not always be easy.

When/what do the children find hard?

SHARING

Show the children the pictures and encourage them to identify the activity in each picture.
Divide the children into three groups, one for each picture, and have them pretend they have to do what their picture shows:
they have to decide what preparations they need to make.
Time permitting, gather everyone back together and share what preparations they each think they need.
Often we want to do something,
- but cannot be bothered to make the necessary preparations
- or start out and get bored
- or we cannot be bothered trying any more.
God made us and loves us. He never gets bored of loving and looking after us.

work out what you will need, and how much it will cost. Otherwise, you might be half way through, and run out of money. Then people would think you very silly.

Or suppose you were a king marching to war. You must first find out if the other king is much stronger, has a much bigger army than yours. No one goes to battle if they know they will be defeated.

That would be very silly.

So too if you want to follow me, you must know what it will mean. You must be prepared to follow me all the way to the end.'

This is the Gospel of the Lord.
Praise to you, Lord Jesus Christ.

ACTIVITIES

> Give out the cross shape cut-outs.

> On them have the children write or draw the way in which they will help Jesus in the week ahead.

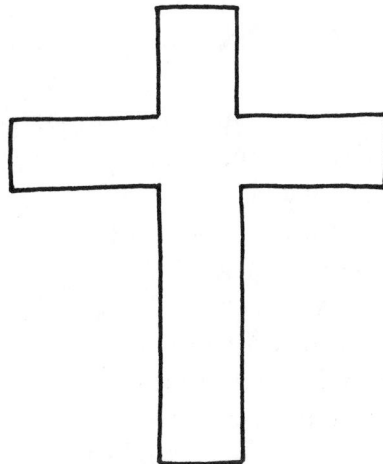

LET HEAVEN REJOICE

VISUAL AIDS

> Two posters, one saying LOST, the other saying FOUND.

> Some lost and found adverts from newspapers.

> Sheep shape and coin shape cut-outs.

WELCOME AND PROCLAIM THE GOSPEL

Say/sing together:

**Alleluia, alleluia!
May God help us see and find
the treasure he has for us.
Alleluia!**

A reading from the Good News given to us by Luke.
Glory to you, Lord.

Jesus says,
'Imagine you were a shepherd with a flock of 100 sheep, and lost one? Wouldn't you go out to look for the one lost sheep, even though you had 99 others?
Wouldn't you search everywhere, even in dangerous places?

DISCUSSION

Who are the two people that Jesus asks us to imagine?
What do they both have in common?
- they both lost something.
What did they lose?
- a sheep, and a coin.
What did they do?
- searched hard and long for it.
Why?
- because it was so valuable to them.

How did they feel when they found what was lost?
- happy, and rejoicing.

How can we get lost from God?
How does God feel?
How does God search for us?
What happens when someone who is lost is found?
- everyone should rejoice with God.

SHARING

Encourage the children to share their experience of losing things:
how did they feel?
what did they do about it?
how did they feel when they found what they had lost?
Today Jesus tells two stories about people who lost things. Listen to what they did.

And then when you found it, what would you do?
You'd put it on your shoulders, and come home again happy.
You'd be so happy you would probably call all your friends together and have a party to celebrate.

Or suppose you were a housewife who had ten coins but lost one. Wouldn't you light a lamp, look in every corner, sweep the whole house out until you found it?
And wouldn't you call on your friends or neighbours to tell them the news?

So too God your Father welcomes back anyone who is lost.'

This is the Gospel of the Lord.
Praise to you, Lord Jesus Christ.

ACTIVITIES

> Have the children mime the two Gospel scenes.
Some can play the part of the sheep.

> Let the children choose either a sheep shape or a coin shape cut-out.

> Have them write or draw on them what they would like God to find them doing during the coming week, so that God and their friends or family will be happy: e.g. 'I will help with the washing up'; etc.

BE A WISE SERVANT

VISUAL AIDS

> Some price tickets with reduced prices.

> An assortment of goods marked half price.

> Price tag shape cut-outs.

WELCOME AND PROCLAIM THE GOSPEL

Say/sing together:

**Alleluia, alleluia!
Jesus was rich,
but became poor for your sake,
so that he could make you rich.
Alleluia!**

A reading from the Good News given to us by Luke.
Glory to you, Lord.

Jesus told his friends this story;
'A rich man once had a very lazy servant, who wasted the rich man's money. The rich man sent for this servant and said
"Because you're lazy and have wasted my money, I'm going to sack you." The servant wondered what he

DISCUSSION

How did the lazy servant make friends?
- by letting people off with half of their bill.

How do we reach our home in heaven?
- by not letting wealth take us over.

How could wealth take us over?
- if we worry too much about getting more
- if we are tied by what we own
- if we worry too much about losing what we have.

Encourage the children to give examples.

SHARING

Have the children look at the goods and the reduced price tickets.

In a shop would the children look first at full price goods? at reduced price goods?

Would they pay the full price if they could get the same thing cheaper elsewhere?

Would you go to a shop where you knew things were dearer?

Today Jesus tells us about a man who needed to make friends quickly. Listen to how he did it.

would do. He wasn't strong enough to dig; he was too proud to beg. Then he had an idea. He sent for everyone who owed his master money, and for every single one, he cut the debt in half. If someone owed 100 measures of wheat, the servant changed it to 50. When the master heard this, he saw how cunningly clever the servant was, and praised him for it.'

Then Jesus said to his friends 'Just as this man used the world's goods to make friends who would give him a home, so you must learn to use things wisely to gain your home in heaven. You must never be the slave of money.'

This is the Gospel of the Lord.
Praise to you, Lord Jesus Christ.

ACTIVITIES

Just as the servant used the things of this world to make sure he had a home, so we must learn to use the things of this world wisely and properly to reach our heavenly home.

We are wise when we share.

> Give out the price tag cut-outs.

> On them have the children write or draw what they will share or give away next week
e.g. give up time to help wash the dishes, tidy the house, etc.
. e.g. give up places in the dinner queue, etc.

LORD, FILL OUR HEARTS WITH LOVE

VISUAL AIDS

> Pictures of poor children.

> A selection of toys or sweets.

WELCOME AND PROCLAIM THE GOSPEL

Say/sing together:

**Alleluia, alleluia!
Jesus was rich,
but became poor for your sake,
so that he could make you rich.
Alleluia!**

A reading from the Good News given to us by Luke.
Glory to you, Lord.

Jesus said to the Pharisees, 'Once there was a rich man, who dressed beautifully, lived expensively, only eating the very best. At the gate of his house lay a beggar called Lazarus. His body was covered with sores. He was so starving that he would have eaten

DISCUSSION

What happens in the story Jesus told?

Encourage the children to give modern day examples of Lazarus and the rich man.

Do they ever behave like the rich man?

- at home, e.g. with little brothers or sisters?
- at school?

SHARING

Show the children the pictures, the toys and the sweets, and encourage them to share their thoughts about these.

Lead them to reflect that
- some people seem to have lots, or even too much
- others have little or nothing.

Today Jesus tells us a story about two people, one of them rich, the other one poor.

---

the food scraps thrown away by the rich man, but no one gave him any. One day the poor man died and the angels carried him to heaven. The rich man also died, but the angels did not take him to heaven. He went to hell. Looking up he could see Lazarus happy in heaven and he said to God
"Have pity on me. I am so hot and thirsty. Send Lazarus to me with a drop of water." But God replied

"You had a good time when you were alive, while Lazarus suffered. Now Lazarus is having a good time. It is impossible for him to cross over and help you.'"
This is the Gospel of the Lord.
Praise to you, Lord Jesus Christ.

ACTIVITIES

> Have the children act out the Gospel story, including examples from their own lives.
> Give out blank paper and have the children write or draw:
either, someone they will share with
or, what it is they will share in the week ahead.

> Recite this prayer together:
**Father, thank you
for all the love and kindness
you have shown towards us.
Help us to be loving and kind
towards others in return.
Father, thank you
for the food we have.
Help us not to be greedy and
wasteful with it.
Help us to share with those who
do not have enough food.**

LORD, INCREASE OUR FAITH

VISUAL AIDS

> Pictures of trees, including an oak tree.

> A variety of seeds, including an acorn.

> Tree shape cut-outs.

WELCOME AND PROCLAIM THE GOSPEL

Say/sing together:

Alleluia, alleluia!
Lord, increase our faith.
Alleluia!

A reading from the Good News given to us by Luke.
Glory to you, Lord.

One day Jesus' friends said to him, 'Lord, make our faith bigger.'

Jesus replied,
'The size of your faith doesn't matter. Even if your faith was as small as the tiniest of seeds, if it is true faith you could say to a fully

DISCUSSION

What did someone ask Jesus for?
- that their faith be increased, made bigger.
How did Jesus reply?

What did he mean?
- that nothing is impossible if only we have real faith.

Every Sunday we are invited to make an act of faith together.
We call it 'The Creed'.
How many children know a Creed?
Go through what the basic Creed statements say about God the Father, about Jesus, about the Holy Spirit, and about the Church.

SHARING

Show the children the pictures and the seeds and encourage them to talk about them:
- about how seeds have within them the power to become plants and even trees.
Show the acorn and the picture of the huge oak.

Could any of the children pick up a tree? The stump of a tree? A little tree?
The roots anchor them very firmly into the ground.

Today Jesus talks about seeds and how to move trees.

grown tree
"Go and jump in the sea!" and it would obey you.'

This is the Gospel of the Lord.
Praise to you, Lord Jesus Christ.

ACTIVITIES

> Give out the tree shape cut-outs.

> On them have the children write their own act of faith, e.g.
  'I believe God made me.
  I believe Jesus died and rose to save me.
  I believe the Spirit gives me life.'

LET US GIVE THANKS TO THE LORD

VISUAL AIDS

> A thanksgiving table arranged with leaves, fruit, flowers, food, etc.
> Pictures of happy children.
> The theme message LET US GIVE THANKS TO THE LORD OUR GOD made out on cards, one word per card (for a large group of children make several sets).
> Gentle music.

WELCOME AND PROCLAIM THE GOSPEL

Say/sing together:

**Alleluia, alleluia!
For all things give thanks,
because that is what God expects
you to do in Christ Jesus.
Alleluia!**

A reading from the Good News given to us by Luke.
Glory to you, Lord.

As Jesus travelled towards Jerusalem, near one of the villages, ten lepers came out to meet him. They did not come too close, but called from a distance,
'Jesus! Master! Take pity on us!'
Jesus replied
'Go and show yourselves to the

DISCUSSION

What happened in today's Gospel?
How many lepers were healed?
How many came back to thank Jesus?
What did Jesus say to the one who returned?
- your faith has saved you.

Who was this leper?
- a Samaritan.

Explain, as necessary, how the Jews despised Samaritans.

Can the children think of any examples of people who are not Christians, but who behave better, more kindly, more lovingly than some Christians?

SHARING

Invite the children to look at the things on the table, and to try and discover the message from the word cards.

What do the children have to be thankful about?
What is there about themselves, their lives, their families for which they want to thank God?

Ask the children to sit quietly (use the soft music to help the atmosphere) and think of what they are thankful for.

In today's Gospel we hear how Jesus healed some people who were sick. Listen carefully to see if any of them say thank you.

priests.'
The lepers set off to do this, but on the way, even before reaching the priests, they were cured. One of them came back to Jesus, praising God at the top of his voice. He threw himself at Jesus' feet and thanked him. Jesus said,
'Were not all ten made clean? Where are the other nine?' To the one leper who did come back, who was a Samaritan, Jesus said,

'Stand up and go on your way. Your faith has saved you.'

This is the Gospel of the Lord.
Praise to you, Lord Jesus Christ.

ACTIVITIES

> Have the children act out the story.

> Give out blank paper and have the children write or draw something for which they are grateful.

NEVER LOSE HEART

VISUAL AIDS

> Pictures of praying hands, of people praying.
> Prayer books, rosary beads.
> Pictures of people involved in tasks which demand perseverance, e.g. musicians, artists, climbers.
> Heart shape cut-outs.

WELCOME AND PROCLAIM THE GOSPEL

Say/sing together:

**Alleluia, alleluia!
God's word is active and alive.
Alleluia!**

A reading from the Good News given to us by Luke.
Glory to you, Lord.

Jesus told his friends, 'When you pray, you must never lose heart.' Then he told this story: 'Once there lived a judge, who was very full of his own importance and not always fair to those who came to him for advice and help. There was a widow who kept coming to him for

DISCUSSION

Who are the people in Jesus' story?
What did they do?
How does the story end?

What does the story tell us about God?
Are there any things that the children find it difficult to persevere with?

Encourage them to give examples, e.g. managing always to remember morning and night prayer, grace before meals, etc.

SHARING

Show the pictures to the children and ask what they mean to them. Invite the children to give examples of when they had to make a big effort to accomplish something. What was it like, having to make an effort? What did it feel like to achieve the goal?

What does it feel like not to succeed? And if we don't succeed the first time, what should we do? - try again . . .

In today's Gospel Jesus tells us about a woman who never gave up trying.

protection against an enemy who was threatening her. When the judge did nothing, the woman came back and asked again. So too the next day, and the next. Day after day she kept pestering the judge for fairness. Finally the judge said "This woman is pestering me to death. I'll give her what she wants and get some peace.'" Jesus said to his friends 'Even the unjust judge gave the woman what she wanted when she kept asking; how much more will God your Father do for you when you ask him.'

This is the Gospel of the Lord.
Praise to you, Lord Jesus Christ.

ACTIVITIES

> Have the children act out the story.

> Give out the heart shape cut-outs.

> On them have the children write or draw something that they find it difficult to persevere with, but that they will make a special effort to do in the coming week.

HAVE MERCY ON ME, JESUS

VISUAL AIDS

> Pictures of two very different men.

> Flag shape cut-outs.

WELCOME AND PROCLAIM THE GOSPEL

Say/sing together:

**Alleluia, alleluia!
God, through Jesus,
grants mercy to all.
Alleluia!**

A reading from the Good News given to us by Luke.
Glory to you, Lord.

Jesus met some people who prided themselves on being good, so he told them this story.
'Once, there were two men who went up to the Temple to pray.
One man was important, a Pharisee. The other man was a tax collector, and no one trusted him.

DISCUSSION

Who are the two men in the story?
- a Pharisee and a tax collector.
Explain, as necessary, that the Pharisees prided themselves on keeping the law as exactly as possible.
The tax collector was collecting the taxes on behalf of a foreign power - the Romans.
How did the Pharisee pray?
- boastfully.

How did the tax collector pray?
- humbly.
The Pharisee thought he did not need God's help;
the tax collector knew he needed God's help.
Are the children ever boastful? If so, what about?
The only thing we should ever boast about is Jesus:
- that Jesus is the greatest; Jesus is my best friend; etc.

SHARING

Show the children the pictures of the two men, and encourage them to make up stories as to who they are, what their work might be, etc.

In today's Gospel Jesus tells us a story about two men, who are very different.

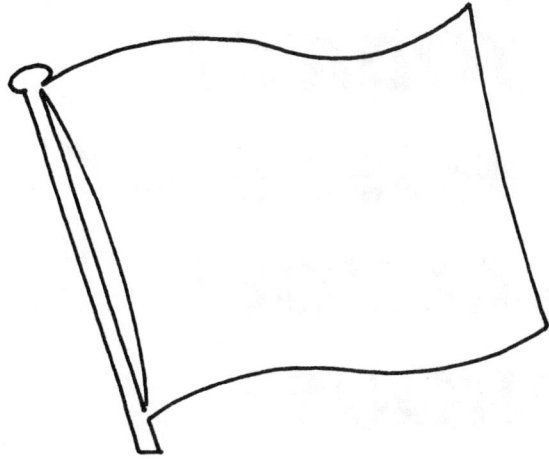

The Pharisee began his prayer this way,
"Lord, I thank you that I am not like the rest of men. I thank you that I am not like this greedy tax collector. Thank you, God, I do everything I should, and much more."

The tax collector stood at the back, and didn't even dare lift his eyes to heaven. This is how he prayed. "God, have mercy on me, a sinner."

Whose prayer do you think God listened to?'

This is the Gospel of the Lord.
Praise to you, Lord Jesus Christ.

ACTIVITIES

> Have the children act out the story, if possible adding modern day examples.
> Have the children sit quietly, and to pray like the tax collector, asking God to forgive them for being boastful.
> Give out the flag shape cut-outs.
> On them have the children write or draw what they want to boast about in Jesus, e.g. 'Jesus is the greatest'.
> Recite this prayer together:
  We rejoice at the victory of God.
  We make our boast in his great name.
  We boast of his goodness.
  We boast of his love.
  We boast of his justice and mercy.

TODAY I MUST STAY AT YOUR HOUSE

VISUAL AIDS

> Pictures of crowds.

> House shape cut-outs.

WELCOME AND PROCLAIM THE GOSPEL

Say/sing together:

Alleluia, alleluia!
Blessings on the one who comes in the name of the Lord.
Alleluia!

A reading from the Good News given to us by Luke.
Glory to you, Lord.

In Jericho lived a man called Zacchaeus, who was rich, but not very big. When Jesus came to Jericho Zacchaeus wanted to see him, but when he arrived the crowd was so big that Zacchaeus could not see a thing. So he ran ahead and climbed a tree. When Jesus reached the tree he

DISCUSSION

What happened to Zacchaeus?

- at first he was curious about Jesus
- he saw Jesus
- he listened to Jesus
- he welcomed Jesus
- he let Jesus change his life.

Jesus calls to us.
What does he ask of us?

- to listen to him
- to welcome him
- to change our lives for Jesus.

In what ways can we change for Jesus?
Encourage the children to offer examples.

SHARING

Encourage the children to talk about their experiences of being in crowds, e.g. to watch a procession go past. What might they do to be able to see?

Today's story is about someone who was too little to see in a crowd.

looked up.
'Zacchaeus', Jesus said, 'come down. Hurry because today I must stay at your house.'
Zacchaeus hurried down and welcomed Jesus joyfully.
Some of the people began to grumble and complain.
'Why has Jesus gone to Zacchaeus' house? Everyone knows Zacchaeus is a sinner.' But Zacchaeus said 'Lord, I'm going to share half of what I have with the poor. And if I've cheated anyone I'll pay them back four times over.'
Jesus said
'Today, salvation has come to this house.'

This is the Gospel of the Lord.
Praise to you, Lord Jesus Christ.

ACTIVITIES

> Have the children act out the story of Zacchaeus.

> Give out the house cut-outs.

> On them have the children write or draw:
either, how they will welcome Jesus in the coming week;
or, a way in which they will change their lives for Jesus.

WE WILL RISE AGAIN

VISUAL AIDS

> Fruit, bulbs, and seeds.

> A bowl and soil.

> Autumn leaves or Autumn pictures.

> Seed shape cut-outs.

WELCOME AND PROCLAIM THE GOSPEL

Say/sing together:

Alleluia, alleluia!
Jesus is the first-born from the dead;
to him be glory for ever.
Alleluia!

A reading from the Good News given us by Luke.
Glory to you, Lord.

One day some people who did not believe we will one day rise again came to Jesus and tried to trick him with a riddle.
'Once there were seven brothers. The first brother married a wife, but died before they had any children. So, according to the law, the second

DISCUSSION

What was the riddle Jesus was asked?
How did he reply?

Go back to the seeds, and talk about the promise of new life that each seed carries.
In us too there is the promise of new life.

This promise is given to us in baptism.

SHARING

Encourage the children to talk about Autumn:
- that the leaves change colour and fall from the trees;
- fruits, berries and seeds remind us that new life will come again after Autumn and Winter.

The promise of new life is in the seeds.

Plant some bulbs and talk about how they will flower in Spring.

In today's Gospel we will meet some people who didn't believe in new life.

---

brother married her. He too died before they had any children. So too with the third, the fourth, the fifth, the sixth and finally the seventh brother all married this woman. They all died leaving no children. Finally, the woman died. At the resurrection whose wife will she be?'

Jesus replied,
'There will be no need for marriage for those who rise to new life, for they will be the same as the angels and children of God.'

This is the Gospel of the Lord.
Praise to you, Lord Jesus Christ.

ACTIVITIES

> Have the children mime the story and the riddle.
> Give out the seed shape cut-outs.
> On them have the children write or draw how they will try to grow in the new life of Jesus
   - by being happy, helping others, sharing, spreading happiness.

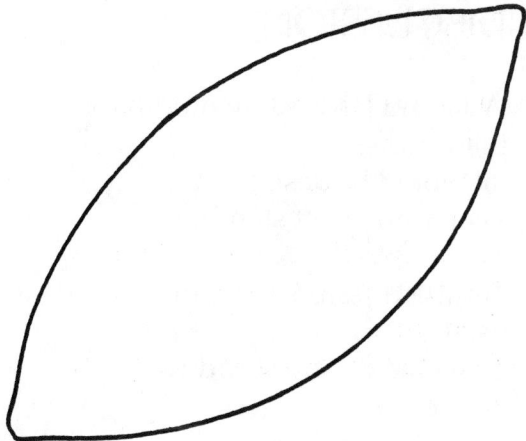

NOT A HAIR OF YOUR HEAD WILL BE LOST

VISUAL AIDS

> Pictures of fine buildings, churches, stonework.

> Some hair.

> People shape cut-outs.

> Quiet music.

WELCOME AND PROCLAIM THE GOSPEL

Say/sing together:

**Alleluia, alleluia!
Lord, come
and make your home in us.
Alleluia!**

A reading from the Good News given to us by Luke.
Glory to you, Lord.

One day when Jesus was in the Temple, some people were admiring its stonework and ornate carvings. They were full of praise for it. But Jesus said,
'All of this will one day
come to an end.
Everything will be destroyed.

DISCUSSION

What did Jesus say would happen to the Temple?
- it would be destroyed
- not a stone left standing.

What did Jesus say would happen to us?
- not a hair of our head would be harmed.

Jesus tells us never to be afraid. No matter what happens, God will always be there to look after us.

SHARING

Show the picture to the children. Encourage the children to talk about famous buildings they have visited. How did they feel about them? What did they like about them? When we visit great buildings, cathedrals, abbeys, we are full of praise for the clever men who built them.

Talk about the various parts of the building we might admire, tower, spire, carvings, etc. But people are more wonderful than any building on earth. People can make buildings, but it is God who makes people. Each person is a home for God on earth.

Not a single stone will be left standing on another. But you are more precious than any building, even this one. God will never allow anything to harm you. Not even a hair of your head will be lost.'

This is the Gospel of the Lord.
Praise to you, Lord Jesus Christ.

ACTIVITIES

> Everybody is afraid of something. Play quiet music and invite the children to speak to Jesus in their hearts and tell him their fears.

> Give out the cut-outs.

> On them have the children write or draw how they want God to keep them safe.

YOU WILL BE WITH ME IN PARADISE

VISUAL AIDS

> Pictures of the beauties of creation: scenery, flowers, animals, fruit, etc.
> Pictures of people of all nationalities.
> Tape of the Taizé chant 'Jesus, remember me'.
> Either, people shape cut-outs; or, heart shape cut-outs.

WELCOME AND PROCLAIM THE GOSPEL

Say/sing together:

Alleluia, alleluia!
Blessed is the one
who comes in the name of the Lord.
Alleluia!

A reading from the Good News given to us by Luke.
Glory to you, Lord.

As Jesus was dying on the cross, a crowd of people gathered to watch. They laughed at him, and made fun of him.
'He saved others', they said, 'If he really is the Chosen One why can't he save himself?'
The soldiers joined in, shouting

DISCUSSION

Who were the people watching Jesus? What were they saying?

Who were being crucified alongside Jesus?
And what did they say to Jesus?
What favour did one of them ask?
And how did Jesus reply?
- Jesus used his power to offer him a place in paradise.

Jesus has chosen to share his power with all who are baptised. He wants us to use this power in the same way that he did: to help others and to bring them home to paradise.

SHARING

Today we celebrate the feast of Jesus Christ our King.

What is Jesus King of? Use the pictures to lead the children to say Jesus is the King of all creation. Because Jesus defeated evil and death on the cross, God has made him King of everything that is living, of everything that is.

Listen carefully to today's Gospel, and we will hear how Jesus began to use his power.

'If you're the King of the Jews, save yourself.'
There was a notice pinned above Jesus' head, which said
'This is the King of the Jews'.

Along with Jesus, two criminals were being crucified. One joined in with the others, making fun of Jesus. But the other said,
'Stop it! We deserve what is happening to us, but this man has done nothing wrong.' Then, turning to Jesus, he said,
'Jesus, remember me, when you come into your Kingdom.'
Jesus replied,
'I promise you, this day you will be with me in paradise.'

This is the Gospel of the Lord.
Praise to you, Lord Jesus Christ.

ACTIVITIES

> Introduce the children to the Taizé chant, reminding them what Jesus promises in reply.
Leave the song playing while the children complete the other activity.

> Give out the cut-out shapes.

> On them, have the children write or draw how they will use the power that Jesus shares with them to make Jesus' promise come true; how they will live their lives by being kingdom people now.

IN THE NAME OF THE FATHER, SON, AND HOLY SPIRIT

VISUAL AIDS

> A large plain cross.

> Cross shape, triangle shape, or shamrock shape cut-outs.

WELCOME AND PROCLAIM THE GOSPEL

Say/sing together:

**Alleluia, alleluia!
Glory be to the Father,
and to the Son,
and to the Holy Spirit.
Alleluia!**

A reading from the Good News given to us by Matthew.
Glory to you, Lord.

It was after the resurrection.
Jesus' friends made their way to the mountain where Jesus had arranged to meet them.
Jesus came up and spoke to them. He said,
'All authority in heaven and on earth has been given to me.

DISCUSSION

What did Jesus ask his friends to do?
- to make all people children of God.

How do we do that?
- by spreading the Good News;
- by baptising them.

In whose name have we to do this?
- in the name of Father, Son and Holy Spirit.

What things do we do in the name of Father, Son and Holy Spirit?
- anything that we start with the sign of the cross, e.g. mass, prayers, meals.

SHARING

Make the sign of the cross with the children, carefully drawing their attention to the words of the prayer.

Today we celebrate the Feast of the Trinity: of God the Father, God the Son, and God the Holy Spirit. Each time we make the sign of the cross we remember three persons in one God.

In today's Gospel we will hear something about God the Father, God the Son and God the Holy Spirit; listen carefully to see what it is.

Go, then, make all people children of God, baptising them in the name of the Father, and of the Son and of the Holy Spirit.
Teach them to do all the things I have told you.
Know that I am with you always, yes even to the end of time.'

This is the Gospel of the Lord.
Praise to you, Lord Jesus Christ.

ACTIVITIES

> Give out the cut-out shapes.

> On one side of the cut-out have the children write or draw what they will do this week in the name of Father, Son and Holy Spirit.

> On the other side:
shamrock or triangle shapes:
make a badge with the names of the three persons on each leaf or in each corner;

cross shapes:
write one of these prayers:
   In the name of the Father,
   and of the Son,
   and of the Holy Spirit.

   Glory be to the Father,
   and to the Son,
   and to the Holy Spirit.

EAT THIS BREAD, DRINK THIS CUP

VISUAL AIDS

> Pictures of the Last Supper.

> Ears of wheat.

> Different kinds of bread.

> Pictures of people sharing a meal.

> Loaf and cup (chalice) shape cut-outs.

WELCOME AND PROCLAIM THE GOSPEL

Say/sing together:

**Alleluia, alleluia!
Lord, give us the living bread
from heaven.
Alleluia!**

A reading from the Good News given to us by John.
Glory to you, Lord.

Jesus says:

'I am the bread of life
which has come down from heaven.
Anyone who eats this bread
will live for ever.
The bread that I shall give is myself,
given that the world may live.

DISCUSSION

In today's Gospel we hear Jesus promise that he will give us special food and drink.

When did he did he keep this promise?
- at the Last Supper when he said
'This is my body; take, eat . . .
This is my blood; take, drink . . .'

When does Jesus give himself for the life of the world?
- on the cross.

What is special about this bread and wine?
- in giving us these, Jesus gives us his very self.

When does Jesus give himself to us to be our food?
- in communion.

SHARING

Encourage the children to give examples of different ways of having meals: schools dinners; parties; picnics; barbecues.

What are the children's favourite meals? Favourite foods?

Explore with children how bread is made from many wheat grains.

Once the ears are ground into flour and made into bread, they can never be separated again.

Jesus says that those who eat the bread of life will never be separated from him.

Anyone who eats this bread
and drinks this cup
has eternal life.
Anyone who eats my flesh
and drinks my blood
lives in me
and I live in him.
This is the bread sent from heaven,
anyone who eats it will live for ever.'

This is the Gospel of the Lord.
Praise to you, Lord Jesus Christ.

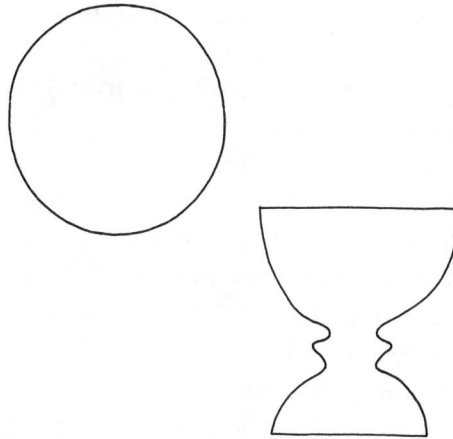

ACTIVITIES

> Give out blank paper and have the children make a poster of the following:

**When we eat this bread
and drink this cup
we proclaim your death,
Lord Jesus,
until you come in glory.**

> Have the children act out the Last Supper.

> Give out the cut-out shapes.

> Have the children colour them, ready for the banquet with Jesus. Then gather them under the double banner 'Eat this bread' and 'Drink this cup'.

DO YOU LOVE ME

VISUAL AIDS

> Pictures of St Peter and St Paul.
> Pictures of the present Pope, and of your present bishop (if possible, with their croziers).
> Have the extract from Paul's letter in an envelope.
> An envelope and paper for each child.

Take the following extract out of its envelope.
A reading from Paul's letter to the Church at Galatia.

You must have heard how at first I was one of those who persecuted the Church. I tried to prove I was better than anyone else by the way I tried to destroy the Christians. But God called me to be his servant, and chose to reveal his Son to me, so that I might preach the Good News to pagans. So I set off at once travelling throughout the world, preaching the Good News.
This is the Word of the Lord.
Thanks be to God.

Stand, and say/sing together:
Alleluia, alleluia!
Happy are those
who are chosen to serve God.
Alleluia!

DISCUSSION

What does Paul tell us in the first part of his letter?
How is the second part different?
What was it that changed Paul?

What did Jesus ask Peter?
What did Peter reply?
What did Jesus ask Peter to do?

We call Jesus our Good Shepherd. Jesus asked both Peter and Paul to do his work.
Our Pope and our bishops are asked by Jesus to carry on his work today. They are shepherds. Point out the croziers, shepherd's crooks.

Do we love Jesus enough to give part of our lives to do his work?

SHARING

Today we celebrate the feast of two very great friends of Jesus; Peter and Paul.
Both of them believed in Jesus so much they gave their lives to him and for him.
Encourage the children to share what they know about Peter and Paul.
Peter was Jesus' first apostle. Jesus named him 'Rock'.
Paul didn't come to know Jesus until after the resurrection. Jesus appeared to Paul and called him to follow him. Paul travelled hundreds of miles, through many dangerous journeys to spread the Good News of Jesus.
Today we have two readings, one by Paul about himself, and one about Peter.

A reading from the Good News given to us by John.
Glory to you, Lord.

Jesus said to Simon Peter,
'Simon Peter, do you love me?'
'Yes, Lord', Peter answered, 'you know I love you.' Jesus said,
'Feed my lambs.' Jesus asked again,
'Simon, do you love me?'
'Yes, Lord', Peter replied, 'you know I do.'

'Look after my sheep' said Jesus.
Then he asked a third time,
'Simon, do you love me?' Peter was upset and so he said,
'Lord, you know everything. You know I love you.'
Jesus said to him, 'Feed my sheep.'

This is the Gospel of the Lord.
Praise to you, Lord Jesus Christ.

ACTIVITIES

> Give out the blank paper (and envelopes), and have the children write letters to Jesus saying how they will work for him.

> Pray together for:
the Pope, your own and all bishops;
for the Church all over the world; especially in those parts of the world where the Church is persecuted and it is hard to work for Jesus.

293

GROW BRIGHT LIKE THE SUN

VISUAL AIDS

> An old shoe.

> A large shopping-bag.

> An old wooden chair.

> Medal shape cut-outs.

WELCOME AND PROCLAIM THE GOSPEL

Say/sing together:

**Alleluia, alleluia!
May we grow brave
in the light of Christ.
Alleluia!**

A reading from the Good News given to us by Matthew, Mark and Luke.
Glory to you, Lord.

Jesus took with him Peter, James and John, and led them up a high mountain to be alone.
Then, as Jesus prayed, he changed. His face grew bright and shone like the sun; his clothes grew as white as light.

DISCUSSION

Who noticed all the ways of growing in today's Gospel?
There was Jesus' face which grew . . . like . . .?
And his clothes grew . . . like . . .?

And what about Jesus' friends?
How did they grow?
- they grew full of wonder; they were full of joy to be there; but also, because it was so special, they grew a little afraid.
So what did Jesus say to them?
-'Don't be afraid.'
Jesus wants his friends to grow in bravery for him.
How can we be brave for Jesus?
- by standing up for doing right;
- by not being naughty, e.g. not pushing in the dinner queue, etc.

SHARING

Using the visual aids, put these riddles to the children: how can a shoe grow? how can a bag grow? how can an old wooden chair grow? Shoes can grow old; shopping bags grow full and heavy; chairs can grow uncomfortable.

And now what about us? How many ways can we grow in a minute?

Suggest a couple of the following to get the children started, and then encourage them to think of more (have the children stand up to act them out): we can grow big; small; floppy; strong; sleepy; etc.

In today's Gospel we hear of a time when Jesus grew in some rather special ways.

Peter, James and John grew full of joy, and Peter said,
'Lord, it's wonderful to be here.'

Suddenly a bright cloud came over them and covered them with its shadow.
And a voice from the cloud said,
'This is my Son. Listen to him.'
When they heard this, Peter, James and John grew frightened. They fell on their faces to hide.

Jesus touched them and said,
'Get up.
Don't be afraid.'
Jesus was telling them to grow brave.

This is the Gospel of the Lord.
Praise to you, Lord Jesus Christ.

ACTIVITIES

> Have the children mime the Gospel, acting out especially the ways of growing.

> Give out the medal shapes.

> Have the children write or draw on them:
'I will win my medal for being brave for Jesus by . . . '.

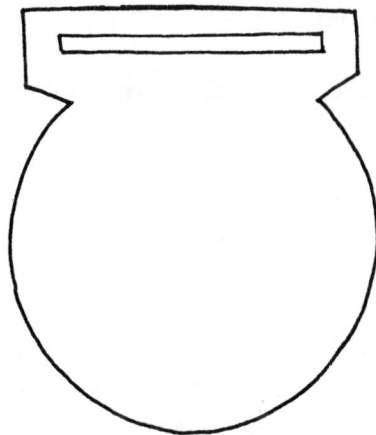

THESE ARE THE PEOPLE WHO SEE THE LORD'S FACE

VISUAL AIDS

> Pictures and books about the saints.

WELCOME AND PROCLAIM THE GOSPEL

Say/sing together:

Alleluia, alleluia!
Come to me if you are weary,
and I will give you rest,
says the Lord.
Alleluia!

A reading from the Good News given to us by Matthew.
Glory to you, Lord.

Crowds of people were following Jesus, trying to see him and hear him speak. When Jesus saw the crowds, he climbed a little hill, where he sat down. His friends joined him, and he began to talk to the people:

DISCUSSION

What did Jesus talk to the people about?
- happiness.

What happens to happy people?
- they are rewarded in heaven.

How did Jesus say we can be happy?

Who are the happiest people?
- the saints in heaven.

SHARING

Encourage the children to talk about their favourite or patron saints.
Which of them are named after saints?
What do they know about those saints?
What is it that made these people saints?
Talk about some of the popular saints.

Do the children think saints are special people?
In fact, Jesus wants us all to be saints, and in today's Gospel he tells us how we can do it.

'Happiness is knowing how much you need God.
Happiness is being gentle.
Happiness is wanting God in your life.
Happiness is longing for what is right.
Happiness is being generous always.
Happiness is putting God first.
Happiness is being a peace-maker.
Happiness is standing up for God.
Happiness is suffering for God.

Rejoice and be glad, your reward will be great in heaven.'

This is the Gospel of the Lord.
Praise to you, Lord Jesus Christ.

ACTIVITIES

> Have the children take it in turns to mime for the others an action related to a particular saint (e.g. Saint Francis feeding the birds; Saint Martin cutting his cloak to share it with the beggar). The child who guesses correctly takes the next turn.

> Give out blank paper, and have the children:
either, write or draw about either their own patron saint, or the patron saint of their church;
or, choose one of the 'Happiness is . . .' phrases and illustrate it;
or, make a badge of their patron or favourite saint.

I WILL GIVE THEM EVERLASTING LIFE

VISUAL AIDS

> A cross depicting the risen Christ, or pictures of the risen Jesus.

> Candles or votive lights (enough for one for each child).

> Easter (Paschal) candle.

> Flower shape cut-outs.

WELCOME AND PROCLAIM THE GOSPEL

Say/sing together:

**Alleluia, alleluia!
The Lord says,
none of those entrusted to me
by the Father will be lost.
Alleluia!**

A reading from the Good News given to us by Matthew.
Glory to you, Lord.

Jesus says,
'Come to me, all you who labour
and are tired and weary,
and I will give you rest.

Learn from me.
I am gentle and humble in heart.'

DISCUSSION

Talk about the children's baptism, how they were given a candle to keep burning brightly.

In baptism we became lights of the world with Jesus.
We keep our lights burning brightly by loving Jesus and each other.

Even though we are only tiny lights, we can still shine brightly.
One day our lights will shine for ever in heaven.

Today we remember the people we love who are now shining like bright stars in heaven with Jesus.

SHARING

Arrange an altar, with flowers, and the Easter candle.
Invite the children to come to the altar and to name someone known to them who has died. Light a small candle from the Easter candle to represent that person.
Explain that the Easter candle represents Jesus, the Light of the world.

Jesus is the light who has conquered all darkness, even the darkness of death.

Those who die are at rest for ever. In today's Gospel Jesus promises rest for his friends.

This is the Gospel of the Lord.
Praise to you, Lord Jesus Christ.

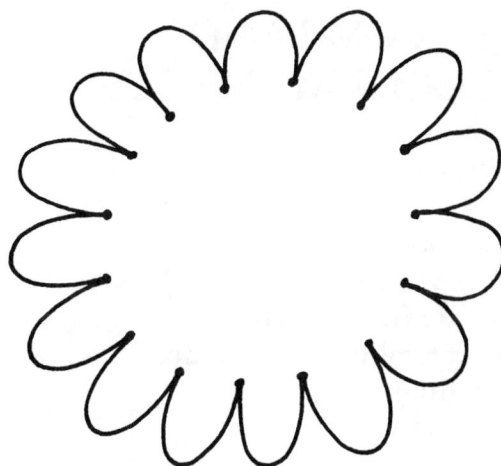

ACTIVITIES

> Explain the custom of making a wreath of flowers when someone dies; that the beautiful flowers remind us of the lovely person who has died; that the wreath is a circle to remind us of the everlasting life that person now has.

> Give out the cut-outs.

> Have the children write on them the names of those known to them who have died.

> Have the children decorate the cut-outs, then gather them into a circular wreath. Put a ribbon on it, marked with the words, 'I will give them everlasting life'.

GOD HAS DONE GREAT THINGS

VISUAL AIDS

> Pictures of Mary appropriate to the particular feast.

> Pictures of mothers and children.

> People shape cut-outs.

WELCOME AND PROCLAIM THE GOSPEL

Say/sing together:

Alleluia, alleluia!
We are ready to do
what God wants us to do.
Alleluia!

A reading from the Good News given to us by Luke.
Glory to you, Lord.

God sent his messenger, the angel Gabriel, to a town in Galilee called Nazareth, where Mary lived. Mary was going to be married to Joseph. 'Rejoice, Mary', the angel said, 'God has chosen you especially.'
Mary did not understand what the angel could mean, and she was

DISCUSSION

Mary said 'Yes' to what God wanted her to do. She lived her whole life for him.
Do the children know of other people who give their lives to God?
Mary said 'God has done great things for me.'
What great things has God done for the children?

Mary said 'My whole life gives glory to God.'
How can the children give glory to God by their lives?

SHARING

Talk through with the children the feast being celebrated, asking them what they know of it.

Have an appropriate song or prayer that can be sung or recited together.

frightened. The angel said, 'Mary, do not be afraid. You are going to have a baby boy. You must call him Jesus. He will be great. He will be called the Son of the Most High.'
Mary replied,
'I am ready to do what God wants me to do.'

This is the Gospel of the Lord.
Praise to you, Lord Jesus Christ.

ACTIVITIES

> Give out the cut-out shapes.

> Have the children colour them to represent themselves.

> Stick the 'people' on to cards, and have the children write what they most want to thank God for about themselves.

> Collect these cards on to a large poster, with the message 'God has done great things for us'.

> Have the children make up a prayer in praise of Mary, using the letters M A R Y to begin each line.

> Mime the Gospel.

THE WORLD IS FULL OF THE GOODNESS OF GOD

VISUAL AIDS

> Fruit, vegetables, flowers (if possible, from the children's gardens).
> Relevant items made by the children.
> Bird, animal, fruit, vegetable and flower shapes.
> Reflective music.
> Empty food containers and decorating materials e.g. crepe paper, ribbons, glue, etc.

WELCOME AND PROCLAIM THE GOSPEL

Say/sing together:

**Alleluia, alleluia!
The world is full
of the goodness of God.
Alleluia!**

A reading from the Good News given to us by Matthew.
Glory to you, Lord.

Jesus says,
'Do not worry about your life and what you are to eat, nor about clothes. Look at the birds in the sky. They don't sow seeds, grow crops, gather in harvests, but they don't starve because your heavenly Father

DISCUSSION

Jesus tells us that God cares for us more than he cares for . . .?
- birds
- lilies.

What do the birds not do?
What do the flowers not do?

So what must we not do?
- we must not worry.

ACTIVITIES

> Give out the cut-out shapes.

> Have the children colour them in, and then stick them on to a large sheet of paper to make a harvest picture or frieze.
A thematic background could be prepared on the paper beforehand, e.g. a large basket, bearing the message

SHARING

Play the reflective music (e.g. Beethoven's Pastoral) to create a calm atmosphere. Ask the children to think of the things in their lives that they are most grateful for. What is it, above all else, that they want to thank God for?
Here is a psalm of praise and thanksgiving:
Response
Give thanks to God for he is good.

For he is God our Father. *R.*
For he works great wonders. *R.*
For he fills the earth with good things. *R.*
For he made the heavens. *R.*
For he made the earth and the sea. *R.*
For he made the sun and the sky. *R.*
For he made the moon and stars of night. *R.*
For he gives us food and drink. *R.*
To God, the Lord of all creation. *R.*

feeds them. Aren't you worth more than they are? And can all your worrying make you any taller? And why worry about clothing? Look at the lilies growing in the field. They never have to work or spin, but not even the most splendid king is dressed as splendidly as they are. If that is how God clothes the flowers in the fields, which are here today and gone tomorrow, won't he look after you much better?

So don't worry and be asking "What are we to eat? What are we to wear?" Your heavenly Father knows all you need.
Set your hearts on God's kingdom, and all these things will be given to you as well.
Don't worry about tomorrow; tomorrow will take care of itself.'

This is the Gospel of the Lord.
Praise to you, Lord Jesus Christ.

'The world is full of the goodness of God'.

> Give the children empty food containers, which they have to decorate and turn into a gift box. Ask them to take the empty box home, and to fill it with good things, which they can then take to a lonely person.

> Introduce the work of CAFOD or OXFAM. There may be a particular project in operation that the children could take part in.